BIG BOOK *of*
WINDOW
TREATMENTS

by Carol Spier and the Editors of Sunset Books
Menlo Park, California

SUNSET BOOKS

Vice President, General Manager: Richard A. Smeby
Vice President, Editorial Director: Bob Doyle
Production Director: Lory Day
Operations Director: Rosann Sutherland
Marketing Manager: Linda Barker
Art Director: Vasken Guiragossian
Special Sales: Brad Moses

BIG BOOK OF WINDOW TREATMENTS was produced
in conjunction with Melnick & Meyer Books, Inc.
Directors: Marsha Melnick, Susan E. Meyer

STAFF FOR THIS BOOK

Creative Editor: Carol Spier
Book Design: Areta Buk/Thumb Print
Developmental Editor: Carrie Dodson Davis
Illustration: Dartmouth Publishing, Inc.
The editors would like to thank Dorsey Adler and the staff at Textile Design Group, Inc.,
New York, NY, for opening their fabric swatch collection to us.

First Printing June 2006
Copyright © 2006, Sunset Publishing Corporation, Menlo Park, CA 94025. First edition.
ISBN-13: 978-0-376-01749-9
ISBN-10: 0-376-01749-X
Library of Congress Control Number: 2006922997
Printed in the United States of America

For additional copies of *Big Book of Window Treatments*
or any other Sunset book, call 1-800-526-5111
or visit us at *www.sunsetbooks.com.*

foreword

Welcome to the world of window treatment design ideas. Window fashions are such an important part of your home's décor—they frame the view, add drama or provide a backdrop to other furnishings, create privacy when needed, and offer a way to add color and pattern. Thoughtfully chosen window fashions enrich the overall ambience of your surroundings. Made in the appropriate materials, they can also establish or enhance your specific decorating style, be it French country, American federal, Victorian, mid-century retro, contemporary, or another.

As you turn these pages you'll find hundreds of illustrations to inspire the way you dress the windows in your home. Even a quick look will make clear the rich array of style options from which to choose. Look a bit more closely and you'll see that combining treatment types—for instance, pairing curtains with shades or blinds—increases these options considerably.

This book is organized in ten chapters. The first is an illustrated glossary of the basic types of window treatments featured in the rest of the book; accompanying each drawing is an explanation of the key characteristics of the depicted treatment. The last chapter is a planning primer to get you started with purchasing (or making, if you are in the do-it-yourself mode) a window treatment; in this chapter you'll find some basic information on measuring a window and selecting fabric. In between are seven chapters devoted to specific window treatment types—draperies and curtains, shades, valances, swags and cascades, cornices, blinds, and shutters and screens—and one chapter featuring ideas for bed curtains and coverings. Within the window treatment chapters, the illustrations are organized first by type of construction and then shown in combination with other treatments, so be sure to look through the book to see the various options for putting different treatments together.

Throughout the book are special features; many of these show ideas for details and finishing touches or demonstrate how different fabrics give various looks to a single treatment. Others shed insight on unusual treatment types or have ideas for creating unique effects. There are also ideas for accessories such as pillows, tablecloths, and ottomans that can be coordinated with your window fashions.

This book is designed to be a source of ideas and inspiration. As you browse or study these pages, perhaps you'll find a treatment that is exactly the style you're looking for. Without doubt, you'll see much to make you think; and we encourage you to mix, match, tweak, revise, and run creatively with the ideas we've presented.

contents

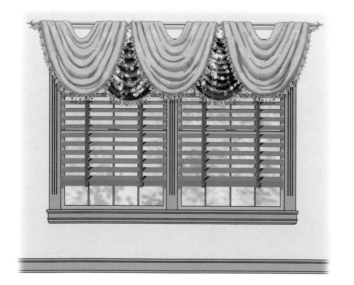

CURTAIN POLE   FINIAL

PINCH PLEAT

PINCH PLEATS are a classic choice for controlling the fullness of draperies. They can be constructed to fold in various ways and may be attached to rings on a pole with finials or to a concealed traverse rod.

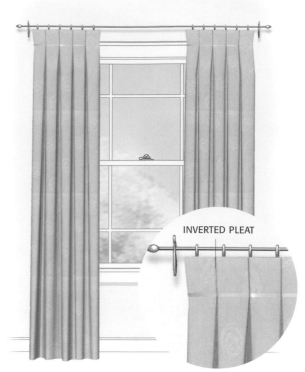

INVERTED PLEAT

INVERTED PLEATS (sometimes called box pleats) provide a flat, tailored control to drapery fullness. They may be sewn closed at the top edge or left unsewn to spring open and add dimension to the top of the panel.

ROD POCKET

A **ROD POCKET** is a channel sewn across the top of a flat curtain; the channel is pushed over the pole until it is condensed to the desired width or until it fills the entire pole.

HEADING

APRON

A **HEADING** is a flat extension of fabric above a rod pocket; when curtains are condensed on a pole, the heading forms a ruffle. The short curtains (above) end at the bottom of the window molding, called the apron.

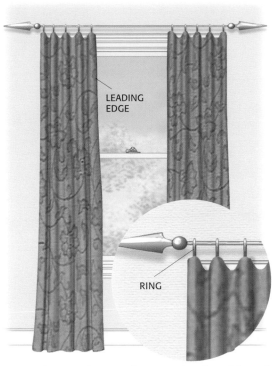

LEADING EDGE

RING

EYELET ON POLE

RINGS provide a simple way to hang curtains; they slide easily across the pole when the leading edge of the curtain fabric is pulled gently. Most large, decorative rings must be sewn to the curtain fabric, although some feature sturdy clips.

LARGE EYELETS set into the top edge of a curtain panel slide over the curtain pole; the fabric above the eyelets forms a small heading. Smaller eyelets are good for lightweight, short curtains.

TAB

WINDOWSILL

TIE, FASTENED IN A BOW

TABS (loops of fabric) sewn at intervals along the top edge of a curtain panel slide fairly easily over a pole. Tabs are sometimes secured with buttons. Short curtains mounted inside a window opening hang best if they end at the windowsill.

TIES sewn at intervals along the top edge of a curtain are essentially the same as tabs, but allow the softer finish of a knot or bow with tails, which may be of any length. Ties may be made of matching or contrasting fabric, or of a trim such as ribbon.

drapery and curtain facts

DRAPERY OR CURTAIN? The terms "draperies" and "curtains" are often used interchangeably for any window treatment that features hanging panels of fabric. There is a difference, though, and it lies along the top edge. Draperies have pleats or gathers that condense their width before they are hung, while the top edge of a curtain is flat until it is hung. To further confuse the issue, there are iterations of both that can—or cannot—be drawn open. Both may be lined, and draperies almost always are. But the name doesn't matter as long as the treatment you order or sew has the look you desire.

Whether drapery or curtain, the top edge of a treatment that hangs from rings, tabs, or ties can be designed so that when drawn open, it folds tightly on itself or drapes and sags—the greater the space between the rings, tabs, or ties, the deeper the sag along the top. If the treatment is significantly wider than the length of its pole, its top edge will sag when closed as well.

Because of the friction of the fabric on the pole, rod pocket curtains are not easy to open or close and are generally designed to be left open or to be held open with tiebacks or holdbacks placed at the side of the window. If you like the look of rod pocket curtains but want your treatment to be easy to adjust, consider gathering the top on shirring tape and hanging it from rings—a ruffle-like heading can be incorporated in this construction.

FABRIC IS KEY TO THE FINISHED EFFECT. Your first thought when choosing a drapery or curtain may be the color or pattern of the fabric, and these are certainly critical. But the weight of the fabric is also important, influencing the way the treatment hangs and making it appear substantial or delicate. The heavier a fabric is, the bulkier it will be when gathered or pulled to the side, so weight should always be considered when choosing a fabric.

FULLNESS GUIDELINES. The fullness of a window treatment varies by style and is expressed as the ratio of fabric width to window width—or, more precisely, to the total width of window plus wall to be covered.

Window treatments with gathered tops—rod pocket or gathered with shirring tape or thread—are usually $2^1/_2$ times as wide as the length of the rod or pole they hang from. Sheers can be 3 times as wide. Heavy fabrics may be only 2 times as wide.

Treatments that are flat across the top and hung from rings or tabs should be at least as wide as the rod or pole so that they cover the window when pulled shut. They usually look better with some fullness.

The fullness ratio for pleated treatments depends on the style and spacing of pleat used—$2^1/_2$ to 3 times the finished width is usual. If the treatment hangs from rings, the top once pleated can be somewhat wider than the length of the pole, but if the top is fixed to a mounting board or on a traverse rod, the measurement must be precise. The thing to remember when planning is that the finished width of the top will be a multiple of the space between the pleats, plus any returns to the wall and overlap at the leading edge.

WIDTH OF WINDOW AND WALL COVERED BY TREATMENT

The width of a treatment that is not pleated is usually $2^1/_2$ times the length of the pole between the brackets or finials—this is the combined width of all panels.

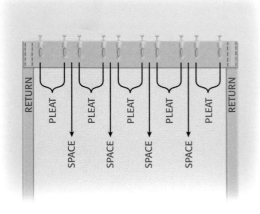

The width of a pleated drapery panel depends on the size and spacing of the pleats. It must be planned so that the sum of the spaces between the pleats equals the width of window and wall to be covered by the closed treatment, and it must also include the return (or overlap) spaces at the edges.

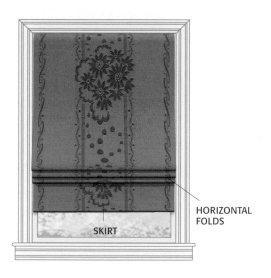

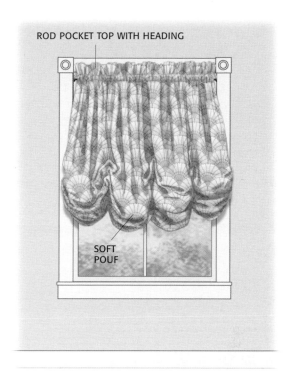

ROMAN SHADES fall into deep, horizontal pleats when they are raised. Depending on their construction and rigging, they may fold crisply or softly, sag in the middle, or fall into tails at the edges. The lower portion forms a skirt if it is not attached to the rigging.

CLOUD SHADES are gathered across the top and rigged to fall into soft poufs when raised. If the bottom edge is gathered onto a dowel, it disappears behind the poufs. If the bottom edge is loose, each pouf falls into a deeper scallop and the bottom edge shows.

A BALLOON SHADE features inverted pleats at each edge and evenly spaced across; these pleats are closed at the top and bottom edges. The shade is rigged behind each pleat and when raised, it falls in neat, tailored poufs that are flat across the front.

A LONDON SHADE is similar to a balloon shade but features just two inverted pleats positioned to create a wide center pouf. London shades are rigged only behind the two pleats, so the outer edges hang down in tails when the shade is raised.

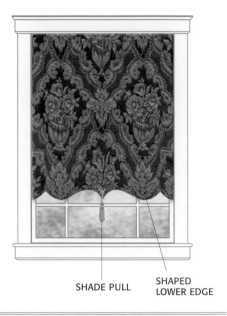

SHADE PULL   SHAPED
LOWER EDGE

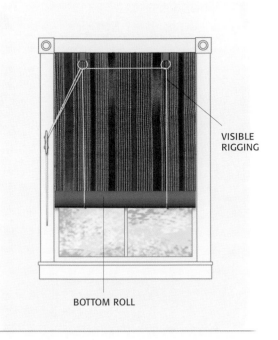

VISIBLE
RIGGING

BOTTOM ROLL

ROLLER SHADES are flat and usually stiff. They roll on and off a cylinder fixed at the top of the window. Decorative shades usually roll off the front of the roller to preclude the back of the shade from showing. The bottom edge may be shaped in various ways.

A ROLL-UP SHADE is similar to a roller shade, but it rolls on and off a cylinder stapled to the lower edge, which is cradled by an adjustable cord that is visible on the front. This type of shade often rolls to the front, revealing the back of the fabric or a lining.

shade facts

INVISIBLE RIGGING. With the exception of roller and roll-up types, a shade is just a fabric panel raised by cords that pass through columns of rings sewn at intervals to its wrong side. Different effects are created when some of the rings are tied together before the cord passes through them, or when the cord does not extend to the bottom edge, or when only a few columns of rings are used. The only rigging on a roller shade is the spring cylinder at the top; the rigging on roll-up shades, while visible, does not provide a means to change their design.

FLAT OR FULL BY DESIGN. Roman shades are the same width as the windows they cover and, when raised, they fall into characteristic horizontal pleats. Cloud, balloon, and London shades are wider than the windows they cover and are gathered or pleated to be that width; when raised, they fall into poufs with distinctive contours. Sometimes the bottom of these wider shades is left loose; when this is the case, the shade falls in bigger curves once raised than when the bottom is fixed at the same width as the top. The drape of these shades is also affected by how soft or crisp the fabric is. Ruffles and fringe can be added to the lower edge of most shades.

MOUNT THEM INSIDE OR OUTSIDE THE WINDOW. Shades of any style may be mounted inside the window or on the molding or wall above it. Make this choice first—it dictates the dimensions of the treatment and the hardware style.

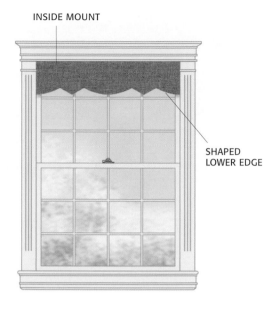

INSIDE MOUNT

SHAPED
LOWER EDGE

OUTSIDE MOUNT

INVERTED
PLEAT

A **FLAT VALANCE** is attached to a mounting board, either inside or above the window and looks like a cornice, especially if it is mounted above the window and returns to the wall at the sides of the board. The lower edge may be straight or shaped.

PLEATED OR GATHERED VALANCES, which can be created in many diverse styles, are often attached to mounting boards, as is this inverted pleat example installed outside the window. Some types work well on rings too.

TAPERED
VALANCE

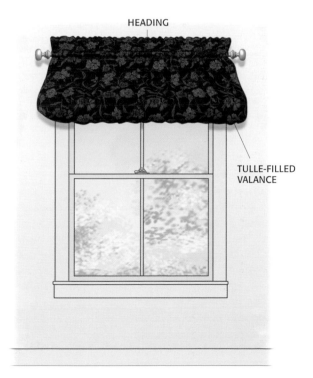

HEADING

TULLE-FILLED
VALANCE

ROD POCKET VALANCES, with or without a heading, may be straight or scalloped on the lower edge, or cut with a curved hemline that tapers at the sides to resemble cascades. They are often trimmed with ribbon, braid, lace, or ruffles.

A **POUF VALANCE** is a tube of fabric with a rod pocket sewn along one long edge. Once gathered onto the pole, it is stuffed with tissue paper or tulle, which gives it permanent volume and keeps the bottom edge soft. A heading is optional.

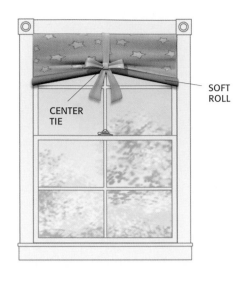

A SCARF VALANCE is a flat topper hung over a curtain pole with minimal draping. It can be shaped in numerous ways, fully double as illustrated, or just a single layer. Sometimes several smaller pieces of fabric are used side-by-side to compose a scarf valance.

A STAGECOACH VALANCE is like a short roll-up shade that is permanently raised. The overall effect may be tailored or soft, depending whether a roller is used at the bottom or if the valance is secured with one center tie or two closer to the sides.

top treatment facts

THREE TYPES OF TOPPERS. Valances, cornices, and swags may all be used both alone and as toppers for other treatments, and the potential design options for them are myriad. Visually, the difference between some styles of valances and cornices is nearly indistinguishable, especially if the valance is mounted outside the window and the fabric returns to the wall. It may just be a matter of who is speaking—one person's cornice is another's valance. A similar naming confusion holds between some valance and swag treatments. The finished effect is more important than what someone calls it, so explore all three to find a style you like. Here are some things to consider:

VALANCES. Structurally, many valances are simply short curtains and others are short shades, so don't be afraid to transfer ideas from one length to the other. Base your choice on the way the valance is used as well as the aesthetic of your overall décor.

While the soft and sometimes frilly look of a rod pocket valance is familiar, nearly any curtain construction can be used short to create a valance. Tab, tie, or eyelet tops can be a good choice for tailored or minimal design styles.

If you like the look of raised cloud or balloon shades, and you don't need privacy or you prefer to darken your windows with a roller shade or blinds, use the cloud or balloon design short—there's no need to invest in the fabric for a long version.

Match valance design to other treatments when appropriate: over café curtains, between curtains that are always open, or over uncurtained windows in a room with curtains elsewhere.

CORNICES. These have a rigid structure that is sometimes masked with draped or pleated fabric (thus the confusion with valances) and are always mounted outside a window. They are usually installed over draperies and generally formal in effect.

SWAGS. Styles vary considerably, with options ranging from controlled constructions fixed to mounting boards or poles to loose arrangements draped over poles or knobs. Fabric choice can affect the formality (or informality) of the finished effect as much as the construction style does. Most swag styles work well alone and over curtains or draperies. Swags are often paired with hanging elements—long cascades or short jabots.

ROD POCKET WITH HEADING

SEWN-ON RUFFLE

ROD POCKET SWAGS offer an informal, easy-to-construct and easy-to-hang alternative to traditional swags. Heading and lower-edge ruffle are optional.

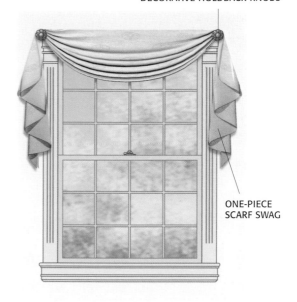

DECORATIVE HOLDBACK KNOBS

ONE-PIECE SCARF SWAG

SCARF SWAGS are made from a single, long piece of fabric that is draped over knobs or special swag holder brackets or wrapped informally over a pole. Styles like the one shown offer an easy alternative to a formal swag-and-cascade combination.

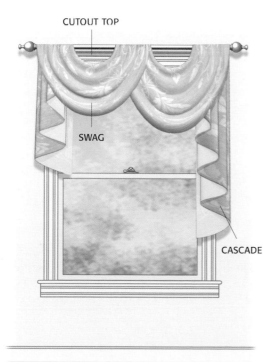

CUTOUT TOP

SWAG

CASCADE

TRADITIONAL SWAGS with cutout tops mounted on a pole and cascades at each end appear to be continuous but are really individual components, each carefully shaped and then arranged as a whole. The number of swags depends on the effect desired.

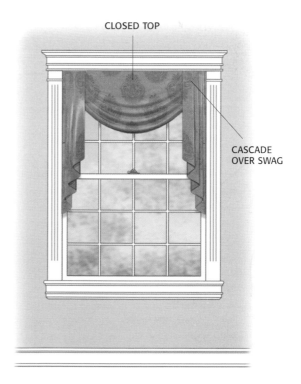

CLOSED TOP

CASCADE OVER SWAG

CLOSED, OR FLAT-TOP, SWAGS are attached to mounting boards, either inside or above the window. Cascades are separate pieces and can be placed over or under the swag, depending on the look desired. One, two, or more swags may be used.

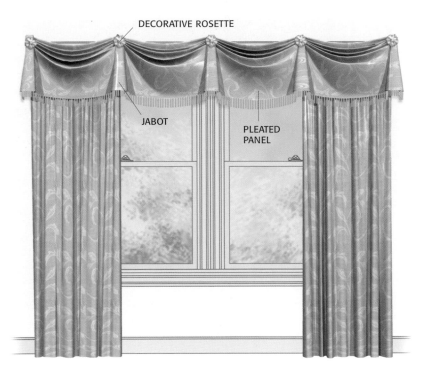

DECORATIVE ROSETTE

JABOT

PLEATED PANEL

SHIRRING

A **SWAG VALANCE** is composed of alternating pleated panels and jabots. The panels differ from true swags in that their bottom edge does not drape all the way up to the top and instead, with the jabots, forms a gently waving line across the window top. They may be tacked to the window trim or a board.

VERTICALLY SHIRRED SWAGS offer an interesting design alternative in traditional colonial or federal décor. Instead of being pleated, these swags are gathered along their sides and vertical center.

BOX CORNICE

SHAPED LOWER EDGE WITH APPLIED TRIM

CORNICES are rigid constructions mounted to the wall around the top of a window; they conceal the top of other window treatments. They may be wood or foam and are often covered with fabric; painted finishes are another option.

The bottom (and sometimes the top and side) edge of a cornice is often shaped, with contours ranging from simple to elaborate or exaggerated, especially in period décor.

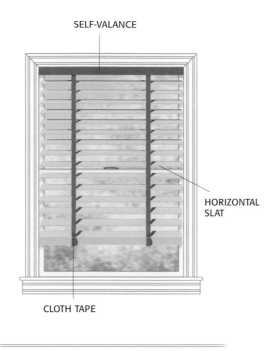

SELF-VALANCE

HORIZONTAL SLAT

CLOTH TAPE

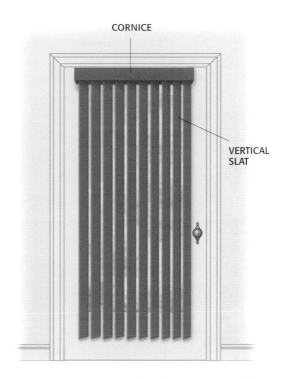

CORNICE

VERTICAL SLAT

HORIZONTAL BLINDS may be mounted inside or outside the window. They are composed of slats (available in several widths) supported between cloth tapes. The slats can be tilted to filter or block the light, and the entire blind may be raised or lowered.

VERTICAL BLINDS are composed of slats strung on cords concealed inside a small cornice; their bottom end is loose. They may be mounted on a door or on the wall above it. They are also appropriate for an outside mount on a window or a glass wall.

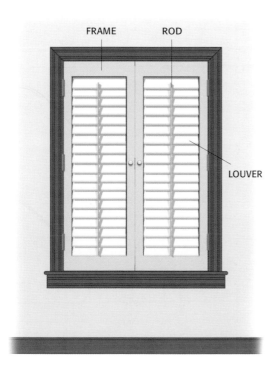

FRAME   ROD

LOUVER

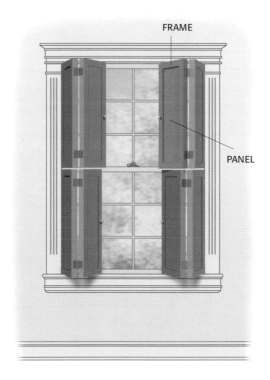

FRAME

PANEL

LOUVERED WOOD SHUTTERS come in sizes appropriate for doors and windows and may be installed singly or in pairs. The louvers are pegged into a frame and attached to a slender wooden rod that acts as a handle to adjust their tilt.

WOOD PANEL SHUTTERS are most often found in period homes, especially those with deep window wells. Sometimes shutters are mounted in tracks so they can slide across the window; shoji screens are also mounted this way.

Inverted pleat draperies, each panel made of three different fabrics, outside mounted on rings

Inverted pleat draperies on a mounting board, draped over holdbacks and trimmed with cord and tassels

Draperies with widely spaced box pleats, affixed to decorative knobs

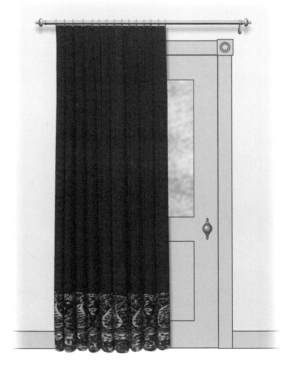

A box pleat panel with a deep band of contrast fabric at bottom, hung on rings over a door

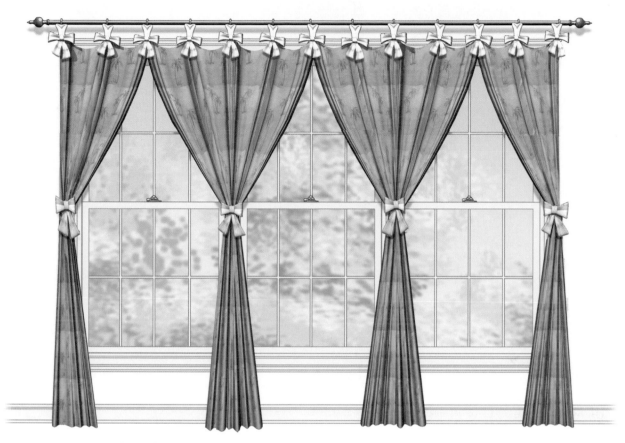

Draperies with widely spaced pinch pleats trimmed with bows, hung on rings on a triple window and tied open individually with coordinating bows

A short pinch pleat panel, inside mounted on a tension rod

Pinch pleat draperies on rings, with a contrasting border on the leading edges

Pinch pleat draperies with rosette trim, on a concealed traverse rod

each pleat style has its own character

Pleats are used to condense the width of fabric at the top of a drapery panel in an orderly manner. There are many styles of pleats, but they fall into two basic categories: those that stand away from the drapery surface and those that fold flat against it; each type releases the drapery fullness with somewhat different effect. All may be hung from rings on a pole or from a concealed traverse rod; the flatter styles may also be attached to a mounting board.

Classic pinch pleats are folded into three loops that are secured 3 or 4 inches below the top of the panel.

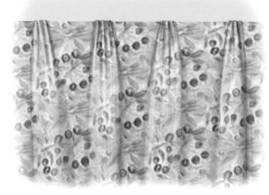

A variant of the classic pinch pleat features three folds of fabric that are secured at the top edge of the panel.

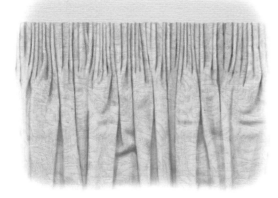

Shirring is created by cloth tape sewn to the wrong side of the drapery; the tape is threaded with parallel cords that are pulled to condense the fabric into fine pleats.

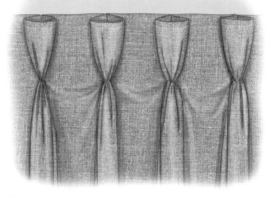

Goblet pleats are a stiffened and stuffed tubular variant of pinch pleats. They crush easily and are usually reserved for stationary draperies.

Inverted pleats, spaced at regular intervals and secured a few inches below the top edge, spring open to form a small tailored heading.

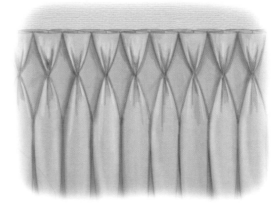

A smocked effect is created when inverted pleats, secured at the top of the drapery and also several inches below it, are folded open and joined where their edges meet.

draperies with shirred tops

Simple shirred draperies on rings, outside mounted and pulled open toward each side of a double door

Shirred draperies on a mounting board, with cord trim at the top and along the leading edge and contrasting tiebacks

Shirred draperies with a heading and tiebacks

A mock swag-and-cascade effect created by extra-short, inside mounted shirred draperies with very high tiebacks

rod pocket curtains

Plain rod pocket curtains, outside mounted on a pole with simple finials

A single, very wide, rod pocket panel with a contrasting vertical border, tied open on one side of a double door

Two pairs of rod pocket curtains with small headings and ball fringe trim, inside mounted one above the other, with tiebacks on the top pair

A wide rod pocket café curtain, outside mounted on a double window, with a heading and a deep ruffle

Short, ruffle-trimmed rod pocket curtains with a heading and ruffled tiebacks

A single, apron-length rod pocket curtain with a heading and a ruffle on the bottom and one edge, tied back loosely

Rod pocket curtains with a coordinated border on all edges

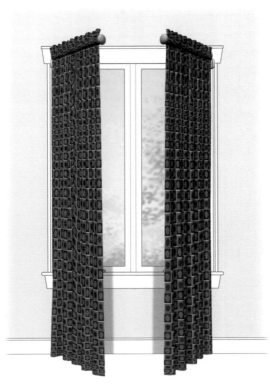

Rod pocket curtains with a small heading, on hinged, swing-out poles

rod pocket curtains

Inside mounted, short, rod pocket curtains with high holdbacks that create a mock swag-and-cascade effect

Rod pocket curtains on a flat rod, with short, ruffle-trimmed sections that drape across the front and tie at the sides

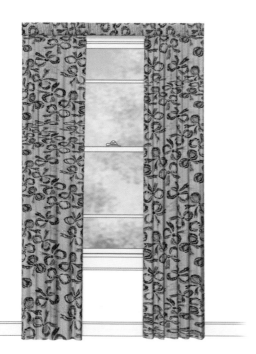

Rod pocket panels separated by a rod sleeve, on a flat rod

Rod pocket panels separated by a rod sleeve, on a round pole with fabric-covered finials

linings and headings are part of the design

Unlike embellishment details such as braid, fringe, tassels, and even tiebacks, which often can be finalized after construction of a window treatment is well underway, lining configuration and rod pocket heading proportions must be chosen before the fabric is cut.

LINE TO THE FACING OR LINE TO THE EDGE. There are two ways a lining may be added to a drapery or curtain panel or to almost any window treatment. In one, the lining is narrower and shorter than the panel and sewn to a margin of the decorator fabric (called a facing) that is folded under along each edge. This method ensures that the lining won't peek out along the edges and be visible on the room side of the treatment even if the panel is pulled to the side with a tieback or holdback. Formal draperies and curtains are usually made this way.

In the other option, the lining is the same width as the panel so the transition from lining to decorator fabric occurs right at the panel edge. With this method, the lining sometimes shows if the construction isn't perfect or when the panel is secured in a holdback or tieback. However, a panel that is lined to the edge may be intentionally folded forward so that the lining forms a contrasting border along its edge, and this is often a desired option.

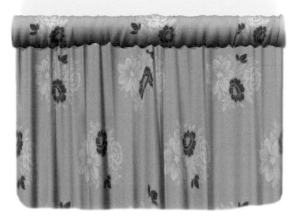

The top of a rod pocket curtain, with no heading

The top of a rod pocket curtain, with a classic heading

The corner of a curtain that is lined to the facings

The corner of a curtain that is lined to the edge

CHOOSE A ROD POCKET HEADING. A rod pocket is a channel in a curtain that slides over a supporting rod or pole. A heading is an optional extension of fabric above the pocket (or below it when there is a lower rod or the treatment is a rod sleeve); the heading forms a ruffle when the curtain is gathered on the rod or pole. If you want to include a heading, consider the overall proportions of your treatment and whether it is hung inside or outside the window, and then choose a heading depth that will appear balanced with the treatment. Consider also the weight of the fabric (flimsy fabrics require extra support or they'll flop over if they are used in deep headings). Shown at right are options for no heading, a classic heading, and a tall heading; very short headings can be effective too.

The top of a rod pocket curtain, with a tall heading

sash curtains move with their window or door

Sash curtains are mounted directly on a window sash or a door, usually with a rod pocket at both the top and bottom edges so they stay taut and don't flutter when the window or door is opened. They're most often used to provide privacy on doors with glass inserts where it would be inconvenient to pull a curtain out of the way in order to pass through the doorway. They can be used on the lower sash of a double-hung window, on casements sheltered from the weather, and on fixed windows.

A sash curtain secured to small rods above and below a glass insert provides no-fuss privacy on an otherwise public door.

A pair of sash curtains covering just three-quarters of the glass creates privacy but leaves a view out casement windows.

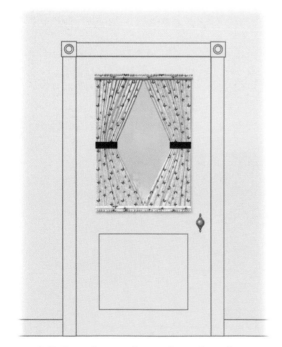

Split hourglass sash curtains soften the look of a door with a glass insert.

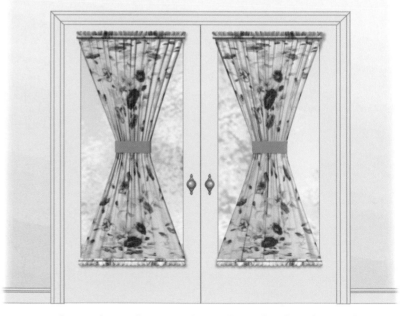

Hourglass sash curtains are a classic choice for glass doors, where they make a pleasant transition from public to private space.

curtains with tab tops

A single panel with contrasting tabs and borders, outside mounted on a door

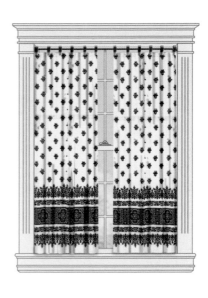

Sill-length tab curtains with a bottom border, inside mounted

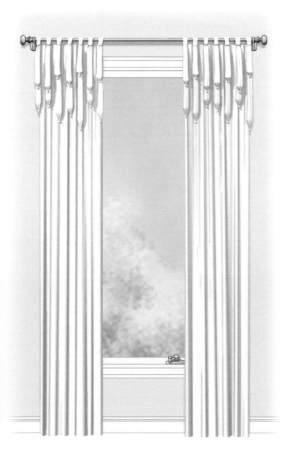

Tab curtains, with a generous, matching, bead-trimmed tie wrapped around each tab

Tab curtains with bound edges, thoughtfully arranged in tiebacks so as to reveal a contrast lining

stylish ideas for arch window curtains

Arch windows may not be as easy to dress as rectangular ones, but consider them an opportunity instead of a problem and you'll find interesting ways to clothe them. You can choose to cover them completely or leave the rounded portion bare. Special curtain rods are available should you decide to cover the top.

Sheer lace curtains, inside mounted and overlapped at the center, are tied back gracefully.

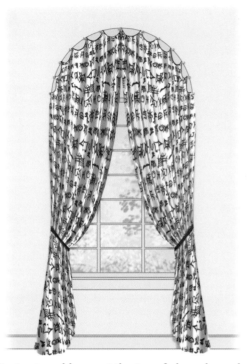

Contrast cord loops at the top of shaped panels slide over hooks placed at corresponding intervals on the window molding.

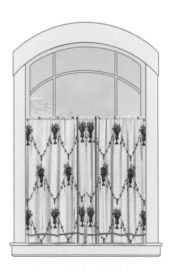
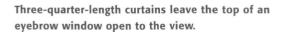

Three-quarter-length curtains leave the top of an eyebrow window open to the view.

A sunburst curtain provides decorative privacy above a permanently pleated Roman shade.

curtains with tie tops

Two tie-top curtain panels hung on each side of a window, with complementary borders and ties

Ties topping pinch pleats on short, curtain-like draperies

Tie curtains with a coordinated bottom border and lining that shows where the top edge drapes forward

Tie curtains hung on decorative ceiling hooks

finials are the jewelry of curtain design

Finials are the caps at the end of curtain poles. While they are sometimes needed to keep the rings from sliding off, they are equally important as design elements that tie your window fashions to other accessories in your décor. Diverse designs are available, from traditional to modern to whimsical, in materials ranging from metal and wood to polymer. They are sized with specific diameters and should be purchased in conjunction with the curtain pole. Here are just a few examples.

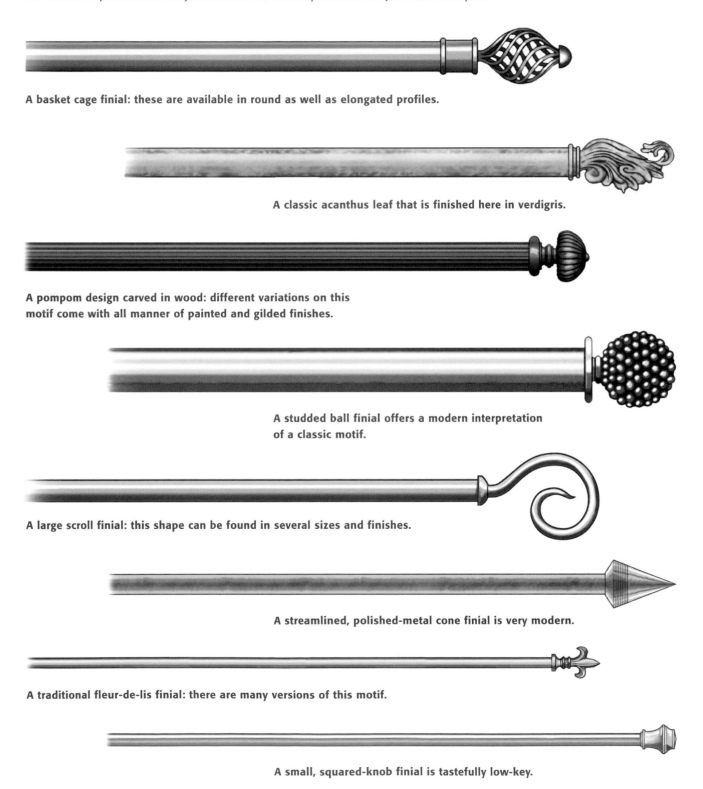

A basket cage finial: these are available in round as well as elongated profiles.

A classic acanthus leaf that is finished here in verdigris.

A pompom design carved in wood: different variations on this motif come with all manner of painted and gilded finishes.

A studded ball finial offers a modern interpretation of a classic motif.

A large scroll finial: this shape can be found in several sizes and finishes.

A streamlined, polished-metal cone finial is very modern.

A traditional fleur-de-lis finial: there are many versions of this motif.

A small, squared-knob finial is tastefully low-key.

curtains on rings

Simple curtains with a wide contrasting border on each leading edge, outside mounted on rings

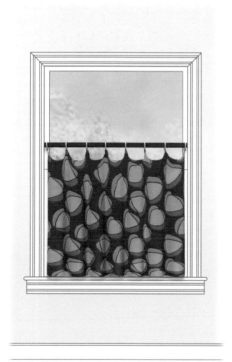

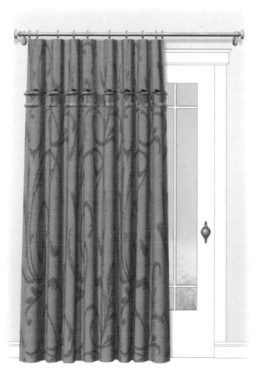

A scalloped-top café curtain on rings, inside mounted on a fabric-covered tension rod

A curtain decorated with tucks across the top, hung on rings

A panel with one edge turned forward and fixed to the second ring to reveal the lining, held open with a tasseled tieback

great edge details

Finishing touches applied to the top, bottom, or leading edges add distinction to drapery and curtain panels. Choices for braid, fringe, ribbon, and similar trims are endless. Structural details such as contrasting bands, tucks, or pleats add simple detail that may be just the thing for tailored or minimalist window fashions; combine them with trimmings if you're looking for a fancier flourish.

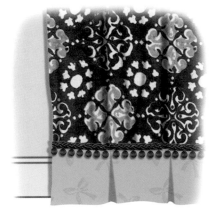

A tailored border with inverted kick pleats is softened by ball fringe.

Paired and single horizontal tucks provide a subtle accent.

Long, luscious, bullion fringe gives an elegant finish to luxurious fabrics.

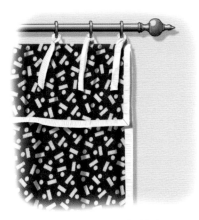

Ribbon adds a flat embellishment; choose a plain color or a pattern.

Classic tassel fringe adds a fancy touch to simple or dressy fabrics.

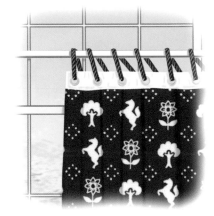

A contrast band laced to a pole through eyelets gives sporty control.

Elaborate braid adds visual weight to the bottom of a generous curtain cuff.

Simple piping stiffens the edge of a curtain heading, enhancing its flare.

curtains with eyelet tops

A short eyelet curtain threaded on a tension rod

An eyelet curtain with deep contrasting borders at the top and bottom

Eyelet curtains with triangular overlays at the top

Eyelet curtains laced onto a pole with decorative cord

fold them back to get an angle on the view

Introduce a diagonal line into your window treatment by folding back one edge of each curtain or drapery panel and securing it at the side. If your panels can't be drawn open at the top, tying them open is the only way to uncover the window; if the panels do draw open, a tied-back look can soften the overall effect. The higher the point of security, the more light, view, and air will be available. If your panels have fullness, tying them back introduces a draped effect; if they are flat, you'll get a tailored look.

One corner of a flat panel is buttoned to the opposite side edge to display the contrasting lining.

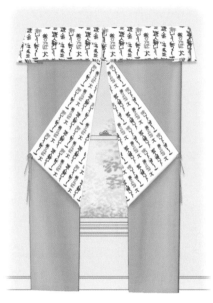

Flat panels have dramatic wings that are tied back to reveal a lining that matches the valance.

Flat panels, with thoughtfully shaped center edges that overlap at the top, are folded back like tent flaps.

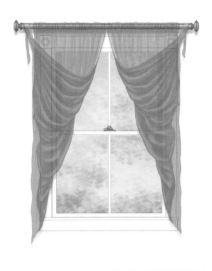

A pair of lightweight, unlined rod pocket curtains is informally draped up and back, with the center edges tied to the pole.

A pair of flat, rectangular panels is pulled back so that the center edges form crisp, jaunty cascades.

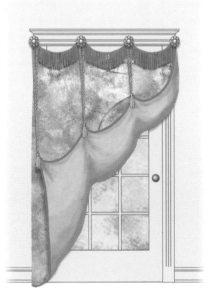

One edge of an elaborate curtain on knobs is folded back and suspended from long, tassel-trimmed cords.

curtains on knobs

Curtains with a top cuff, looped onto knobs on the window molding, trimmed with ball fringe and tasseled tiebacks

Wide panels draped and tacked to the top molding on a narrow window, with big bows covering the tacks

A panel topped by loops of decorative cord that slip over knobs on the window trim, with a tasseled tieback

Wide panels tied onto knobs on a triple window, with the leading edge of each left loose to drape like a cascade

sheer fabrics soften the look

Windows dressed in transparent and translucent fabrics give a soft, often imaginative touch to a décor, especially if the fabrics are arranged to overlap so the light is filtered with varied intensity. Sheer fabrics come in many colors, often with embroidered embellishment, and thoughtful use of hem shadows or trims will further enhance their effect. These treatments are most effective in daylight and don't provide privacy; supplement them with opaque shades.

A single, inside mounted rod pocket panel with a flounce top cuff is tied in the middle with a simple sash.

The layers of a double curtain crisscross as they are tied to opposite sides of the window.

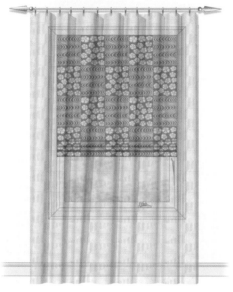

In a whimsical reversal of the norm, a sheer curtain on rings hangs in front of a Roman shade.

One edge of a single rod pocket panel is fixed to the opposite side of the window and drapes into a small cascade.

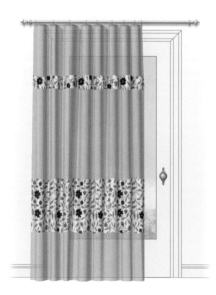

Opaque inserts in a sheer panel play with the view and cast interesting shadows on the interior.

A flat panel is doubled over a pole; then one lower corner of the front layer is lifted and tied to the pole at the opposite top corner.

layered draperies and curtains

Paired curtains hung one in front of the other on separate poles and tied back individually

Pairs of pinch pleat draperies hung one in front of the other and pulled apart to make a double frame for the window

Ring curtains, each featuring a narrow scallop-edged panel in front of a plain panel

Tab curtains, each made with a narrow panel layered over a wider one

draperies and curtains with cuffed tops

A panel with ties topping a fold-down cuff that reveals the contrasting lining

A cuff incorporated in the inverted pleats at the top of drapery panels

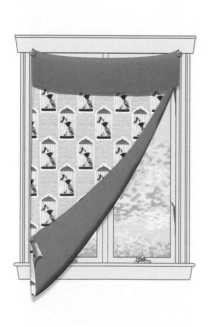

A fold-down cuff on a flat curtain that hangs from a knob at each top corner

A deep, pointed, and tasseled cuff applied to the panel before rings are sewn to the top

A cuff with a shaped lower edge, applied to the panel before the rod pocket is sewn

A flounce cuff, formed when an extra-tall rod pocket heading folds forward

A fringe-trimmed cuff, incorporated in the pinch pleats at the top of the panel

A very deep, shaped, fringe-trimmed cuff on a wide panel that drapes between knobs, paired to flank a triple window

great tieback details

Whether you repeat the drapery materials, add a contrast, or introduce an embellishment, you have numerous options for tieback design. When choosing, look for something that will complement the design and be in scale with the overall proportion of the window treatment. Cord tiebacks with attached tassels are widely available, and some readymade curtains come with coordinated tiebacks; for custom-made treatments, you can commission whatever strikes your fancy.

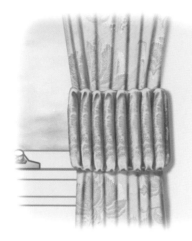

A tall, ruched tieback echoes the effect of a rod pocket on a flat rod.

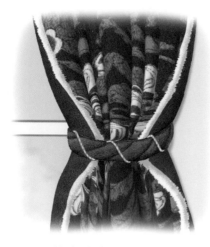

Diagonally folded fabric wrapped with cord makes an unusual tieback.

A double-cord tieback with two big tassels adds a classic, elegant finish.

The fabric choice dictates whether a braided tieback is dressy or informal.

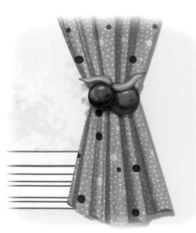

Fake fruit added to a cloth tieback brings a bit of whimsy to short kitchen curtains.

A cord loop extending from a button to a holdback reveals the contrasting drapery lining.

Patchwork tiebacks are a natural choice for country décor.

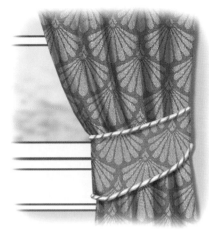

Decorative cord dresses up a plain, contoured tieback.

Wire-edged ribbon tied into a big, multi-loop bow holds its shape well.

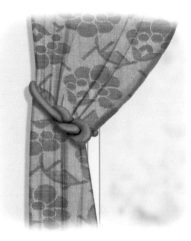

Fabric-covered jumbo cord tied in a knot adds a tailored finish.

Edge a shirred tieback with matching or contrasting piping.

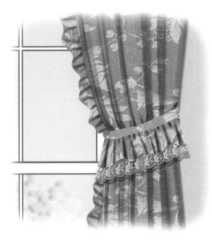

Ruffled tiebacks are the perfect accompaniment to ruffled curtains.

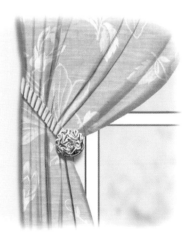

A soft choux rosette complements the gathered fabric of a narrow ruched tieback.

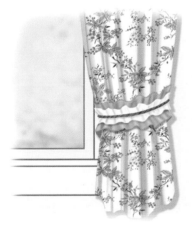

Accent a small, two-layer, double-ruffle tieback with decorative cord.

A sash tied into a jaunty bow with tails makes a pretty yet simple tieback.

draperies and curtains over shades

Curtains and an attached cloud shade, overlapped before the rod pocket is sewn

Pinch pleat, cuffed draperies over an inside mounted cloud shade

Eyelet curtains over a plain, inside mounted roller shade

A single box pleat panel, tied back over a roller shade

Flounce-cuff panels, tied into columns, over outside mounted roller shades with a scalloped lower edge

Shirred draperies passed through long, high tiebacks, over a Roman shade that changes from crisp to soft

Rod pocket curtains over doors fitted with crisp Roman shades

Curtain on rings over a soft, tailed Roman shade

great ruffle details

Depending on their fabric and proportions, ruffles can be elegant and sophisticated, quirky, crisp, or—of course—soft and sweet. They may match or contrast with the rest of the window treatment, be single or multi-layered, pleated or gathered with or without a heading, and may be embellished with ribbon or other trims. They follow a curve well, so they're a good choice for shaped edges.

A very deep, gathered ruffle drapes softly from the edge of a curtain.

A two-layer, gathered ruffle of moderate depth adds a jaunty frill.

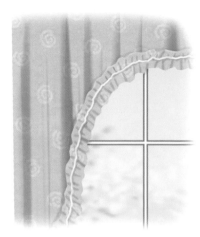

A small ruffle with a petite heading works especially well along curves.

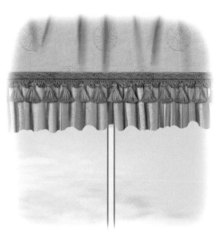

A gathered ruffle gains sophistication when topped by tassel fringe.

A deep sawtooth gives an intriguing finish to a frill of crisp fabric.

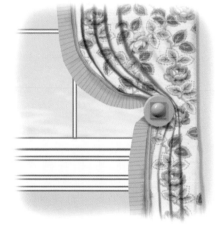

Small, crisp knife pleats march with poised precision along a drapery edge.

A shallow, inverted pleat ruffle springs open with crisp dimension.

A serpentine ruffle creates a double scallop embellishment.

draperies and curtains with valances

An inside mounted rod pocket valance over sill-length curtains

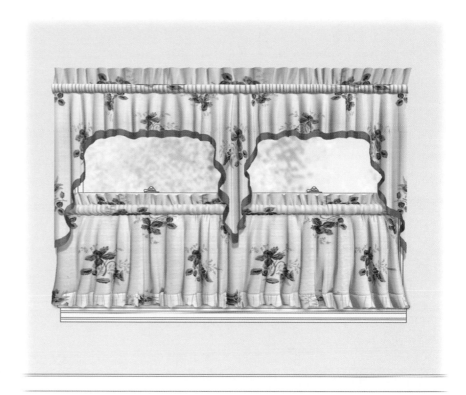

An outside mounted rod pocket valance with tapered hemline over café curtains

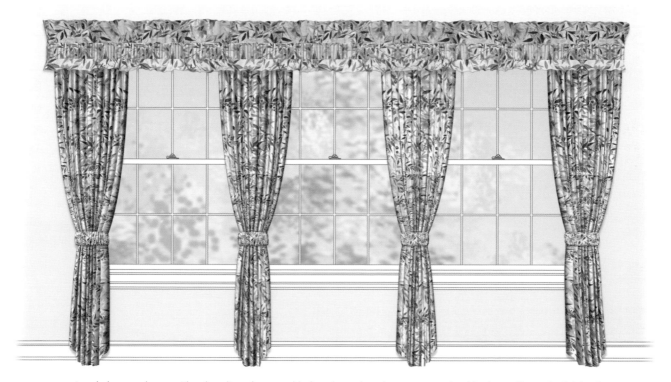

A rod sleeve valance with a heading above and below the rod pocket, over panels with sleeve-like ruched tiebacks

draperies and curtains with valances

Tab curtains separated by a tab valance

A scalloped and pleated valance, on rings, over tied-back panels

An inverted pleat valance on a mounting board, over panels

A ruffle-trimmed triangular scarf valance over panels

A valance of overlapping, tasseled, triangular pieces on a mounting board, over panels with tiebacks

A rod pocket cloud valance with ruffles, over panels with a contrasting border

A deep, box pleat valance framed with jabots and hanging tassels, on rings over panels with tiebacks

A scalloped, box pleat valance on a mounting board, over panels

A shaped-hemline, gathered valance over a swag and panels, with a roller shade under all

drape them high or low for different effects

Curtains and draperies that don't pull open can be swept off the window by various means. They can be draped over holdback knobs or brackets, wrapped by tiebacks, or even rigged on the wrong side with cords passed through a series of small rings. The effect depends somewhat on the type of device; but more important is where it is placed, and how the fabric is arranged in it.

Holdbacks or tiebacks placed close to the floor give long draperies a gentle and serene, yet formal, look.

The exuberant, double drape of this cornice-topped treatment is created by cords rigged diagonally, in two lines, across the back of the curtains.

Short curtains tied back slightly less than half their length above the sill have a fresh, country-cottage look.

A single panel arranged in a generous drape though a tieback high on one side looks graceful and casually sophisticated.

Ruffled panels tied back high above the floor with modest draping have a traditional and intimate appearance.

A single panel, held to one side at the windowsill under a classic swag and cascade, is softly formal.

draperies and curtains under swags and cascades

Short curtains under a ruffle-trimmed rod pocket swag

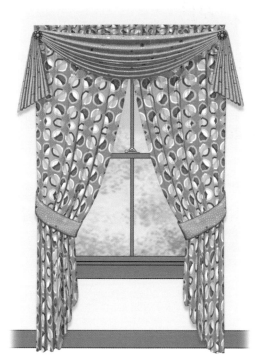

Rod pocket curtains with tiebacks, under a scarf swag draped over decorative knobs

Curtains, each topped with a shawl swag and cascade, all on rings, with tiebacks anchored on decorative knobs

Tab curtains and a matching scarf swag, with tabs and binding in contrasting fabric

Cutout swags with cascades and a center jabot, over rod pocket curtains and a covered flat rod

A double swag with upswept center and cascades, over tied-back panels

Draperies on a triple window, topped by traditional swags with short cascades, and framed by large bows with very long tails

Draperies under an unequal triple swag with cascades

Traditional pleated cascades over a swag,
over contrast panels with tiebacks

Draperies under a double cut-out swag
with asymmetric cascades

Gathered cascades topping a swag valance,
over panels; all edged with contrast trim

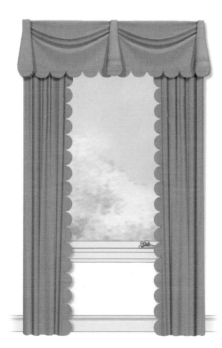

A swag valance with a scalloped hemline,
over panels with scalloped leading edges

great embellishment ideas

It's the embellishments—the buttons, rosettes, cord, and bows added as finishing touches—that provide the points of difference between one curtain and another of similar construction. Keep the scale of your embellishments in balance with the room and the curtain or drapery they enhance, and consider that trims with contrasting colors will be more prominent than those with hues that match the fabric. Here are just a few examples, ranging from very simple to somewhat complex.

Large, tailored buttons accenting inverted pleats

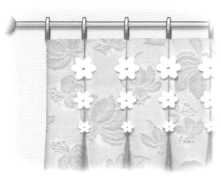

Trios of buttons in graduated small sizes trimming inverted pleats

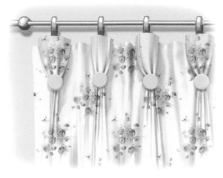

Fabric-covered buttons embellishing extra-full, soft goblet pleats

Tabs, each made from a different fabric and fastened to the curtain with a button

Tabs, each buttoned through a ring instead of riding directly on the curtain pole

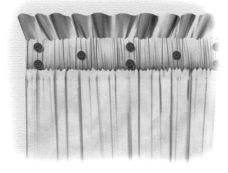

Small pompoms cut from ball fringe decorating the shirred section below a heading

Small, ribbon-loop rosettes at the base of classic pinch pleats

Whimsical rosettes fashioned from brush fringe, trimming a tabbed, bordered panel

Crisp bows accenting the base of pinch pleats that stand above the curtain top

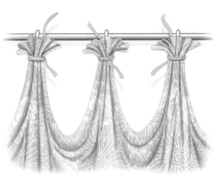

Simple cloth ties wrapping informal pleats pinched at regular intervals along the top of a curtain

A tailored bow with very long tails over panels hung between swags with short cascades

Two strands of decorative cord draped between knobs at the top of an inverted pleat drapery

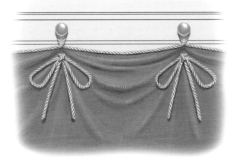

Delicate cord bows sewn below loops at the top edge of a curtain

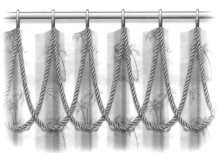

Lengths of cord crisscrossed and sewn to alternating rings along a curtain top

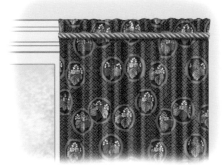

Jumbo cord covering the gathers on a stationary panel affixed directly to the wall

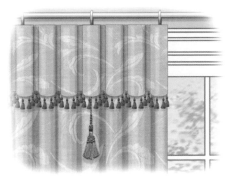

A single, very large tassel accenting a deep, inverted pleat top cuff

draperies and curtains under cornices

A border-covered box cornice topping matching stationary border panels that hang in front of fuller drapery panels

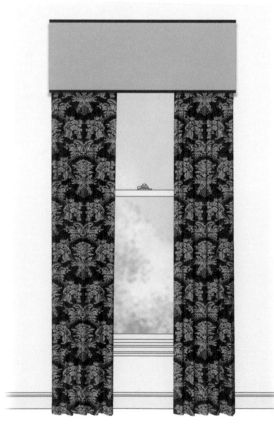

A tall box cornice edged with decorative cord, over panels

A slender padded and upholstered box cornice, over panels

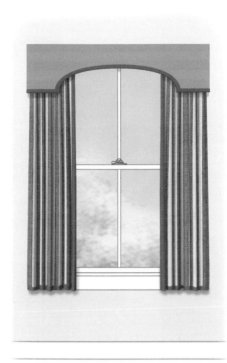

A classic, shaped cornice over short panels, both with contrasting trim

A wood cornice trimmed with crown molding, over panels with fringed leading edges

A cornice with shaped sides and lower edge, over panels

A ribbon-embellished skirted cornice with a shaped, painted wood top, over panels

An elaborate skirted cornice with point overlay, swag, and tasseled cascades, over layered panels with tiebacks

great pillow ideas

Throw pillows with thoughtfully designed details add a sophisticated touch to upholstered furniture. To keep your décor unified, cover pillows in the same fabrics used to dress your windows or in complementary colors or patterns.

A channel-quilted, solid-color pillow cover with contrasting tassel fringe over the flange

A chunky round pillow with a patterned top, solid sides, and contrasting ball fringe

A tapestry envelope-style pillow cover with ball fringe outlining the flap

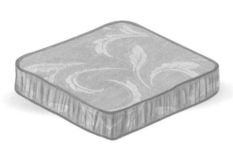

A damask boxed pillow cover with shirred sides and coordinated piping around the perimeter

A solid-color boxed pillow cover with small welts pinched and stitched around the edges

A two-tone, large-print cover trimmed with contrasting cord and a small tassel at each corner

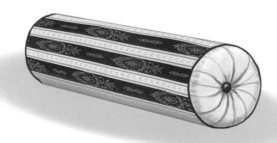

A bolster with a figured stripe covering the sides and solid fabric at the ends, with coordinated piping and covered button accents

A cord-edged, print-covered rectangle with a fringe-trimmed damask cummerbund wrapping the center

draperies and curtains over blinds and shutters

Simple curtains on rings, over louvered blinds

Box pleat draperies, affixed with decorative knobs and trimmed with cord and tassels, over louvered blinds

Pinch pleat draperies over wood panel shutters

Curtains on rings, each draped with a tassel-trimmed scarf valance, over louvered shutters

fabric is key to the look

Most curtains and draperies are just big pieces of fabric varied only by subtle construction details. So what makes a drapery suitable for a formal, informal, traditional, or modern décor—or for a public or private part of your home? The fabric and trimmings from which it is made. Consider how different these simple curtains under a flat valance look with a change of materials and small details.

Fabric patterned with a formal motif such as this swagged bouquet suits a traditional home.

Bold, graphic fabric paired with solids in the same hues has a contemporary, yet classic, effect.

With a juvenile print and contrasting ruffles, the same treatment is right for a pretty nursery.

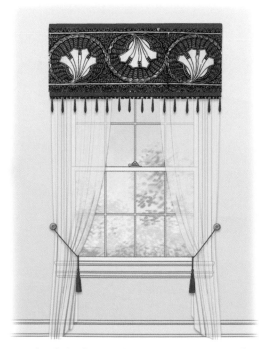

For an eclectic look, try a border fabric—in your favorite period style—with drop fringe over sheer panels.

draperies and curtains over sheers

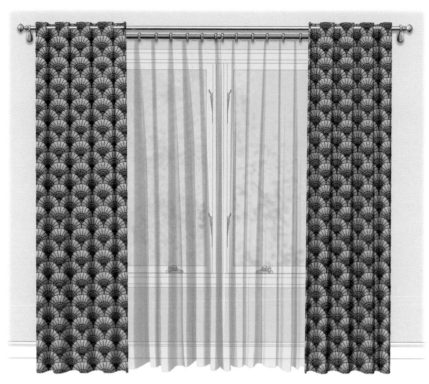

Eyelet curtains over sheers on rings

A swag-topped asymmetric arrangement with a bishop-draped panel opposite a sheer panel

A rod pocket curtain pulled to one side with a tasseled tieback, over a sheer, tailed cloud shade

A gathered valance and panels, with complementary scalloped edges, over tightly pleated sheers

roman shades

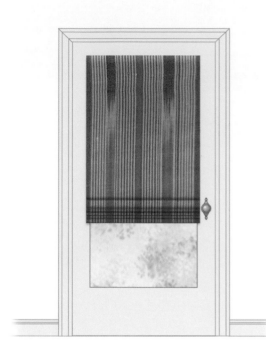

A classic Roman shade, mounted on a door

A Roman shade with a border on the vertical sides, mounted outside the window

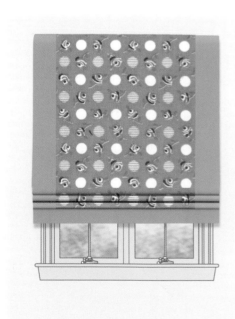

A Roman shade with a wide border on the vertical sides and as a skirt, mounted outside the window

A top-down Roman shade, which lifts from the top edge

A pair of skirted Roman shades, mounted inside the window

A lightly padded and vertically quilted Roman shade

A half-sheer, half-opaque Roman shade with a small skirt

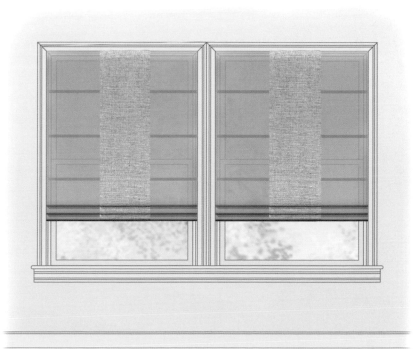

A pair of Roman shades made of sheer fabric with a vertical opaque middle section, with the slats making shadows on the sheer sections

roman shades

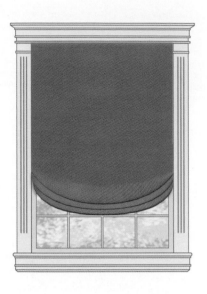

An inside mounted Roman shade, rigged only at the sides so it drapes softly

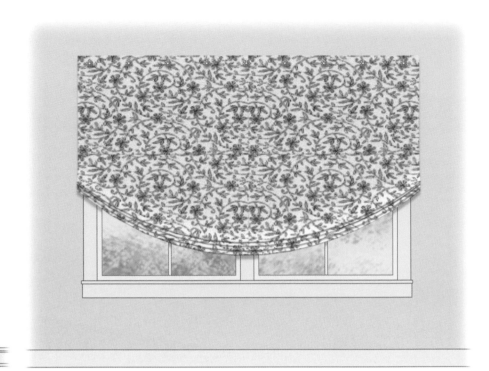

A wide, side-rigged Roman shade, outside mounted, with decorative knobs across the top

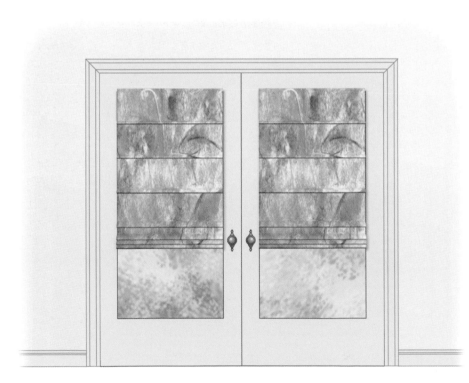

A pair of Roman shades with dowels inserted in pockets on their face, mounted on doors

A hobbled Roman shade, which is constructed so that the face is covered with permanent soft folds of fabric

distinctive roman shades

Handsome as the basic Roman shade is, a small tweak to its typical construction can transform it from a classic window dressing to one that feels especially fresh and contemporary. Here are six unusual Roman shade variations.

A small, inverted vertical pleat gives extra softness to tiered Roman shades made in coordinated fabrics.

Crisp horizontal pleats give way to soft ones with tails for a quirky, yet formal, Roman shade design.

A contrast band along the sides and over the center rigging gives bold import to a Roman shade fan variant.

The lower edge of a soft Roman shade falls into two scallops when cradled by a loop of ribbon that passes through rigging on the shade back.

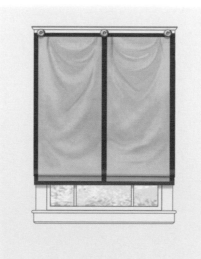

Narrow, contrasting bands edging the shade and in the center make a graphic statement that is softened by small vertical pleats at the top.

Deep folds form when café rods threaded through the shade back are lifted into brackets on the window molding.

roman shades

Roman shades rigged in the center only, causing their pleats to fall into a fan shape, inside mounted on a double window

A soft Roman shade with rigging inset from the edges so the sides fall into tails

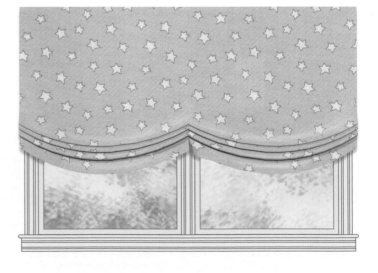

A tailed Roman shade, mounted with buttons across the top, with coordinated fabric in the bottom pleats

A wide, soft Roman shade with a skirt, outside mounted and rigged at the sides and center only, on a double window

cellular shades are modern and discreet

Also called honeycomb shades, cellular shades are topped with a self-valance and feature small, hollow, accordion pleats. When fully raised, they occupy very little space. They are available in numerous colors, patterns, and a variety of materials.

A classic cellular shade makes a clean, simple, window covering.

Versatile top-down/bottom-up rigging allows you to cover or expose both the top and bottom of the window.

A cellular shade in a fan configuration can be custom-ordered for the top of an arch window.

Cellular shades add fuss-free privacy to stationary window treatments like rod pocket curtains.

When top treatments are used without curtains or drapes, consider a cellular shade to block the sun or ensure privacy.

cloud shades

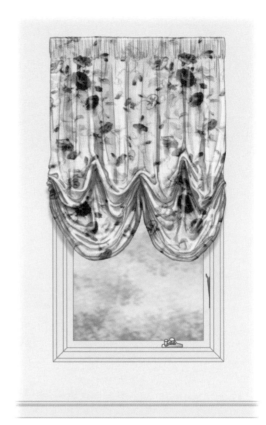

A rod pocket cloud shade, rigged at the sides and center so it falls into two poufs, mounted inside the window

A cloud shade with two large poufs that are each divided into two smaller poufs, on a flat rod

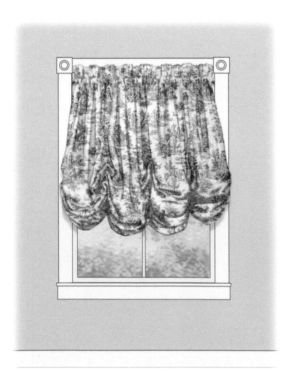

A rod pocket cloud shade with four poufs and a heading

A rod pocket cloud shade with a center pouf that is smaller than its side poufs, outside mounted

A rod pocket cloud shade, rigged to fall into five poufs with staggered heights

An inside mounted, gathered cloud shade, rigged to fall into a large pouf and tails, trimmed with tassel fringe

A tailed cloud shade with two poufs, gathered onto an outside mounted board topped with jumbo cord

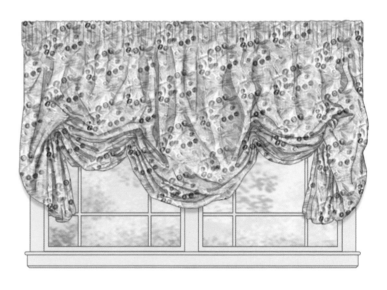

A shirred, tailed cloud shade with three poufs at staggered heights and no trim, outside mounted

fabric is key to the look

Of course, the kind of shade you choose (cloud, Roman, balloon, London) has a considerable effect on your overall décor, but it's the fabric from which a shade is made that sways it from formal to casual or from one design style to another—say, from French provincial to fifties retro. Consider how different a classic cloud shade looks when interpreted in different fabrics and trimmings.

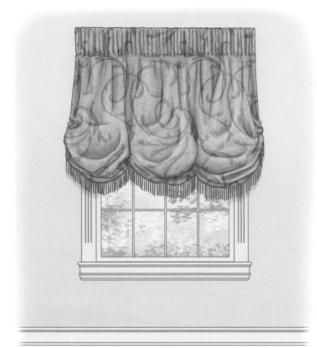

Tone-on-tone damask in a swirling pattern with matching fringe suits a formal décor.

Choose sheer lace fabric with a tiny contrast ruffle for a boudoir or beach house—add mini-blinds for privacy.

Use informal, coordinated fabrics to border the shade with a deep top band and lower ruffle.

For a girl's room, try a delicate, allover floral fabric and add sweet bows with swagged tails across the top.

cloud shades

An outside mounted, shirred cloud shade with a small heading, skirted with one pouf and tails

A skirted rod pocket cloud shade, with rosettes trimming the peaks between the poufs and tails

A rod pocket cloud shade, with a heading and a deep ruffle on the lower edge

An inside mounted shirred cloud shade, with a tiny crisp ruffle on the lower edge

great pillow ideas

Being small and usually simple in shape, throw pillows can be dressed as little works of art without breaking your decorating budget. Here are some ideas for mixing and arranging fabrics on pillow covers to maximize their graphic impact.

Assorted fabrics with a shared palette in a four-patch, quilted pillow cover

A bold print set off by a fold-over solid cuff and contrasting piping on a loose pillowcase

A tailored sham with a richly colored center framed by a lighter flange and scalloped fringe

Floral print side extensions wrapped and tied over a solid-color pillow

A bandana print square framed by decorative cord and a coordinated, solid-color ruffle

A pretty motif cut out as an oval and framed by rickrack on a small, solid-color rectangular pillow

A rectangular pillow cover featuring a border cut from a print fabric and framed by a coordinated solid color

A bolster cover made from coordinated print and damask fabrics, with a contrasting lining in the tied ends and cord and tassel trim

A graphic square-in-square design in solid colors, tufted in the middle with a covered button

A four-patch pillow cover with an uneven stripe in alternating horizontal and vertical orientations

A pyramid pillow with a whimsical scalloped cuff on one side and a big tassel accent

A simple, diagonally divided pillow cover made from two vivid, solid-color fabrics

A saw-tooth flange of deep solid blues framing a lighter blue center pillow cover

Earth-tone ribbons woven to make the top of a boxed pillow cover and accented with small beads

A solid-color bolster cover with a decorative, zigzag-edged button placket made in a woven ikat fabric

A rectangular pillow cover wrapped with a cummerbund, in print fabrics related by circular motifs and warm colors

balloon shades

A classic, outside mounted balloon shade, constructed with three poufs

A balloon shade with five narrow poufs, lowered to the windowsill

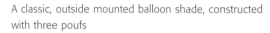

A pair of balloon shades featuring pleats closed with small appliqués, outside mounted on a double window

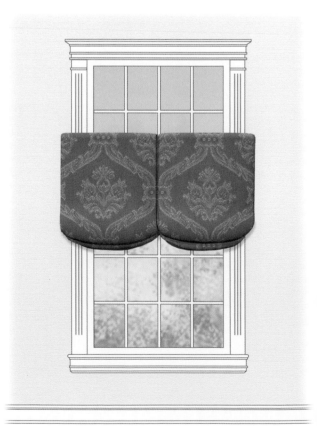

A balloon shade with two wide poufs, mounted to expose the top portion of a tall window

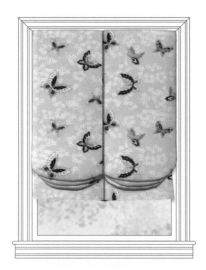

An inside mounted, skirted balloon shade with two poufs

A skirted balloon shade variant, featuring pleats released at the lower edge

A balloon shade trimmed with long fringe

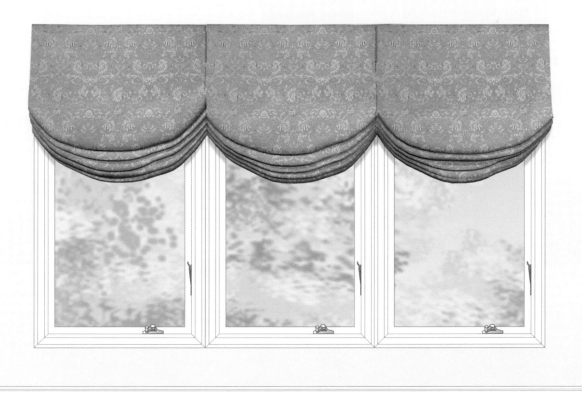

A trio of balloon shades with one pouf each, outside mounted on a triple window

stylish ideas for arch window shades

Windows with a rounded top are fine candidates for shades. Most types of shades can be contoured to follow the shape of the window. And, where sunlight or complete privacy is not an issue, a shade with a straight top installed below the arched area can be a handsome option.

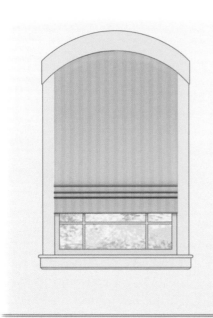

A skirted Roman shade gives tailored privacy in an eyebrow window.

With its deep curvy poufs, a cloud shade complements a window with a half-circle top.

A roll-up shade mounted below a half-circle window keeps the architecture in focus.

A London shade adds simple softness below a curved window top.

A flexible curtain rod makes a wide cloud shade a fine option for a pair of casement eyebrow windows.

london shades

A classic, outside mounted London shade

A pair of floor-length, inside mounted London shades, which form especially generous poufs when raised

A London shade variant, featuring two poufs pleated over flat side sections

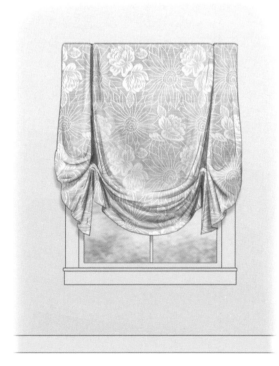

A skirted London shade

great embellishment ideas

Perhaps because the lower edge is so often at eye level, the finishing touches added to a shade make a tremendous contribution to its overall appearance. Even small details like the style of a shade pull or scale of a tassel are worth thought. And, because shades are relatively small as window treatments go, you may be able to splurge on a trimming you'd forego on something more expansive.

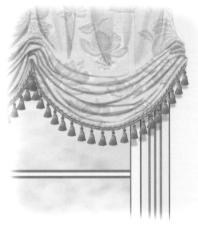

Tassel fringe in the same color as the shade it trims

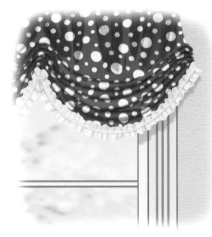

A tiny ruffle, gathered along its middle, on a cloud shade hem

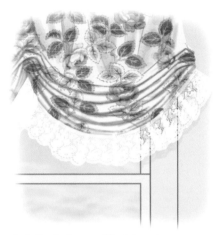

A delicate lace ruffle trimming a cloud shade hem

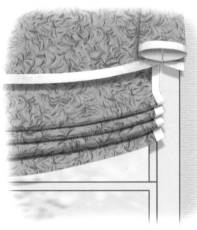

Contrasting trim on the intersecting angles of a Roman shade and companion valance

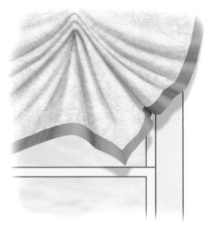

Bound edges outlining a skirted Roman shade

A coordinated skirt bordered with narrow ribbon on a Roman shade

Brush fringe, on the straight lower edge of a boldly patterned shade

Onion fringe on braid, decorating the curved edge of a flat shade

Buttons closing the vertical pleats on a balloon or London shade

A stenciled design decorating a roller shade with a scalloped edge

A bow nestled above the pleats on a tailed cloud shade

An interesting tassel threaded onto the rigging of a roll-up shade

Jumbo cord along the top of a cloud shade, tied in a knot at the corner

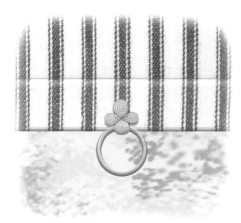

A coiled cord appliqué securing a simple ring shade pull

A tassel shade pull hanging from a metal appliqué

An ornamental metal shade pull

roller shades

A plain roller shade, mounted outside the window

A pair of inside mounted roller shades, with a rod threaded through tabs at the bottom edge

Roller shades, with a shaped bottom edge trimmed with braid

A roller shade with a broad inset bottom border and large tassel pull

A roller shade with the lower edge divided into one large and two small scallops, trimmed with ribbons and bows

A simple roller shade trimmed with braid and fringe at the lower edge

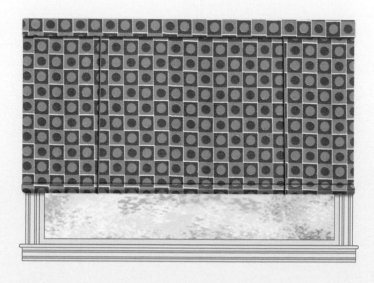

A wide roll-up shade, outside mounted with a self-valance

An inside mounted roll-up shade

hemline contours give roller shades an edge

Roller shades may begin as nondescript rectangles enlivened only by the fabric they're made of, but changes to the shape of their hemlines add the elegance, interest, and punch that make them a good fit for diverse decorating styles.

Alternating large points and scallops, with a center point

Three large scallops, with the center one lower than those on the sides

A large zigzag edge

A delicate scalloped edge

Quirky, unequal zigzags

A bold scalloped edge

Alternating large points and scallops, with a center scallop

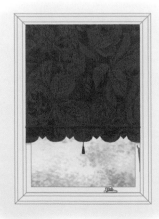

Alternating small points and scallops, with a center scallop

shades under valances or swags

A roller shade under a rod pocket valance, both outside mounted

A pair of inside mounted roller shades, under a double scarf swag

Roller shades with a shaped lower edge, in a double window under a single rod pocket valance with top and bottom headings

A roller shade with braid at the lower edge, under a swag topped by gathered, fringe-trimmed cascades; all outside mounted

shades under valances or swags

A fringe-trimmed roller shade under a balloon valance, both outside mounted

A cloud shade with two poufs, under a cord-trimmed flat valance

A skirted cloud shade, topped by an inverted pleat valance with frog trim

Soft Roman shades under a grand swag valance on a triple window

A Roman shade raised high under a deep flat valance, both inside mounted

A slatted Roman shade, inside mounted under a scarf swag that is arranged in poufs at the top corners

A skirted Roman shade under a small wooden valance, both mounted inside the window

A wide, hobbled Roman shade, under a wide, floor-length scarf swag

great roller shade and valance pairings

If a raised roller shade leaves your window looking underdressed, consider adding a complementary valance. Use the same or coordinated fabric for both pieces, and add trim or play with stripes and borders to create an effect that is pleasing whether the shade is raised or lowered.

Contrasting borders and tassels, duplicated not-quite exactly, make a balanced pairing.

Decorative braid ties a plain shade to a valance with a fancier shape.

Perfectly aligned stripes unify a roller shade and flat valance.

Perpendicular, inset wide borders make a graphic pairing on a simple shade and valance.

Braid and tassel fringe at the shade hemline make it good company for a more complex, pleated valance.

Stenciled motifs turn this shade and valance pair into a bedtime story.

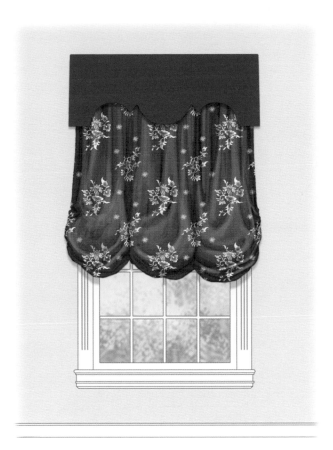

A cloud shade with three poufs, outside mounted under a cornice with a reversing scalloped edge

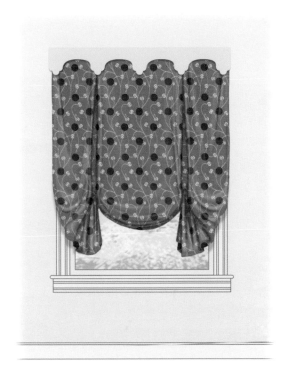

A London shade, outside mounted under a diminutive multi-arch cornice

A tailed Roman shade under a shaped cornice, both featuring a narrow complementary border

A roller shade with an inset border under a box cornice and floor-length draperies

austrian shades festoon with a flourish

An Austrian shade is a cloud shade variant, with the fabric drawn up in columns of permanent gathers to which the shade rigging is attached. As a result, the entire surface is softly draped when the shade is lowered, and extravagantly draped when it is raised. They are most effective made of sheer or lightweight fabric, are sometimes used floor-length on window walls, and tend to create a dramatic finish.

Installed solo, an Austrian shade provides a soft, not-so-formal effect.

An Austrian shade in a low-key fabric makes a modern partner for plain curtains on rings.

An Austrian shade is a natural fit under a period cornice.

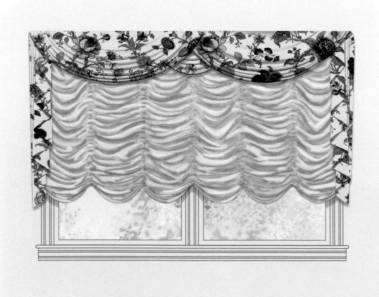

For a very dressy effect on a wide window, complement a triple swag and cascades with an Austrian shade.

shades with sheers

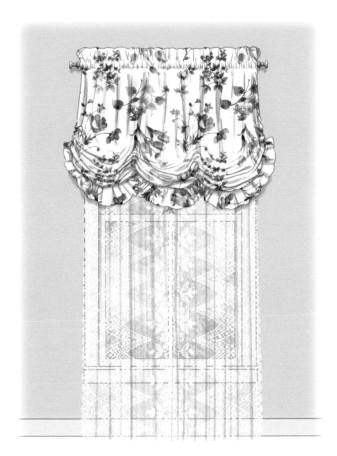

A ruffled, rod pocket cloud shade over floor-length sheers, both mounted outside the window

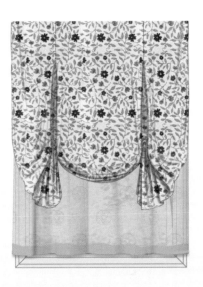

A London shade over sill-length sheers, both mounted outside the window

A skirted Roman shade, inside mounted under crisscrossed flat, floor-length sheers

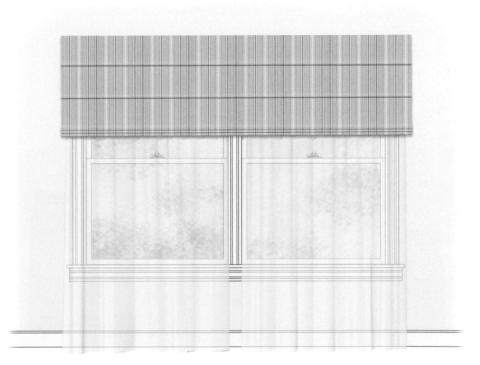

A wide, slatted Roman shade, outside mounted over floor-length sheers

valances

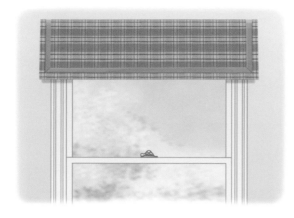

An outside mounted flat valance, with a ribbon
border inset from the edge on three sides

A tall flat valance trimmed with decorative cord,
braid, and ball fringe

An arched flat valance trimmed with decorative
cord on the lower edge

An inside mounted flat valance with a narrow
contrasting border along the zigzag lower edge

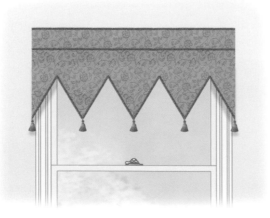

A deeply pointed flat valance trimmed with cord
and small tassels

A flat valance with a scallop-and-point lower
edge and complementary cord

An inside mounted flat valance, with half and full scallops spaced along the lower edge

A scalloped flat valance, featuring a vertical stripe composed of two fabrics and tassel fringe

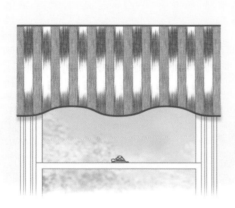

A flat valance with reversing curves on the lower edge

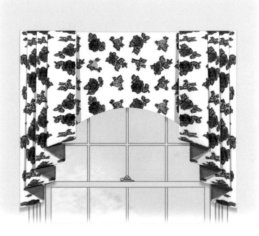

A gently arched flat valance topped with matching pleated cascades

An outside mounted flat valance with long, flat tab overlays, on a double window

A flat wood valance with a contoured edge, fancifully painted to mimic a swag and cascades

pleated valances

An outside mounted valance with a center inverted pleat

A valance on a double window, featuring a pair of inverted pleats centered over each window

A simple, evenly divided, inverted pleat valance

A valance with inverted pleats at the ends and center, with handkerchief points inside the pleats

A valance divided into two large scallops, with inverted pleats at the ends and center, and braid trim

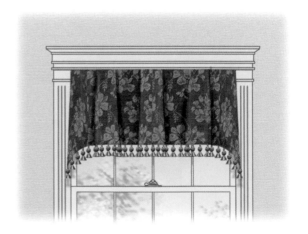

A box pleat valance trimmed with tassel fringe along the curved lower edge

A valance with a pair of box pleats at each end, trimmed with cord and fringe

An inverted pleat valance with a coordinated border on the boldly pointed lower edge

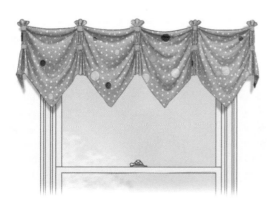

A whimsical, pinch pleat valance with a pointed lower edge and standing pleat tops

A boldly scalloped pleated valance, topped with cascades

A scalloped valance with bell-style box pleats and contrast lining, on a double window

A box pleat valance with a tapered hemline at the sides

great edge details

Chances are the lower edge of a valance is clearly in view, making it a good candidate for fringe or a ruffle. When you're choosing these embellishments, consider how they will look against companion curtains and when silhouetted by daylight.

A fringe of crisscrossed tape and balls is elegant when pierced with light.

A very petite ruffle enhances a scalloped hemline.

A diminutive, pleated ruffle complements a boldly pleated valance.

A double ruffle with a contrasting layer adds sophisticated softness.

Individually attached feathers create an eclectic fringe.

Scalloped fringe makes a soft, pretty, yet not too fancy, edging.

Tassel fringe on braid adds an airy flourish to a curving edge.

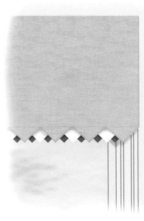

A border of overlapping triangles provides a tailored, graphic finish.

gathered and shirred valances

A shirred valance with narrow ribbon trim on the lower edge, mounted outside the window

A double-skirted valance gathered onto a flat top band, with coordinated trim

A tapered valance gathered onto a curved mounting board, with a heading, small bows, and fringe

A tapered valance gathered more tightly at the sides than in the center

Lightly gathered, tassel-trimmed triangles of fabric mounted on a board inside the window

A deep, shirred valance with a multi-point, tasseled hemline, mounted on a board outside the window

rod pocket valances

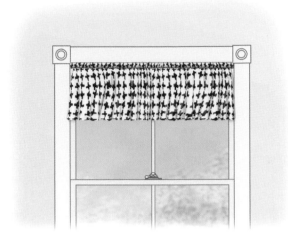

A simple rod pocket valance with no heading, mounted inside the window

A rod pocket valance with a heading, mounted outside the window

A rod pocket valance with a heading, trimmed with dense fringe

A nearly flat rod pocket valance, featuring a pointed hemline trimmed with long fringe

A rod pocket pouf valance with no heading

A rod pocket pouf valance with a heading

A very short rod pocket valance on a flat rod, with a heading and skirt of equal length

A tapered rod pocket valance, with ribbon threaded below the heading and tied in a bow

A tapered rod pocket valance with no heading and short tails

A rod pocket valance tapered so that tails hang at the ends and in the middle of a double window

A rod pocket valance on a double window, with a short scallop in the middle and short tails at the ends

A tapered rod pocket valance with a deep center scallop, tassel fringe, and no heading

use cord and braid to accent and outline

Valances have a strong horizontal presence at the top of a window, and often all that's needed to finish them is a subtle touch of cord or braid. Most cord and braid accents are purely decorative, but some are integral to the structure of the valance.

Simple knots tied in cord and strategically placed on box pleats

Cord used to secure and frame the top of a gathered valance

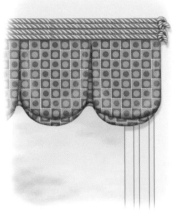

Adjacent double rows of cord, finished with knots

Narrow borders and cord that repeat one tone from a print fabric

Fabric-covered cord along an intricately shaped edge

Bands of braid and ribbon on overlapped pieces

Woven braid inset above a curved lower edge

Cord that coordinates with the braid above a contrasting border

valances with tab, tie, or ring tops

A tabbed flat valance made of diamond shapes that create a pointed lower edge

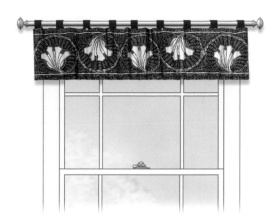

A simple tabbed valance with moderate fullness

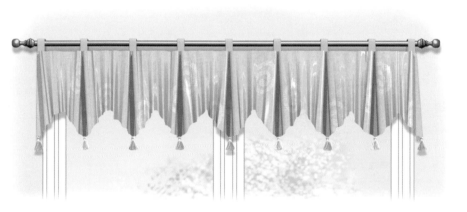

A tabbed valance featuring an inverted pleat below each tab and a pointed hemline with tassels

A tie-top valance with a narrow coordinated border on all edges

A pinch pleat valance on rings, trimmed with braid and fringe

A deep valance on rings, featuring small box pleats and longer cone jabots with tassels

fabric is key to the look

There's no reason to discard or favor a particular valance shape because you think it is suited only to a formal or casual décor. The simplest flat valance will look elegant if made in gorgeous silk or velvet, while many complex valances will take on a charming informality in muslin. Consider, for instance, how various fabrics change the effect of this inverted pleat, scalloped valance.

A traditional, large floral motif, centered on each section, gives a classic or period look.

Bold-figured stripes running horizontally across the valance and coordinated curtains have a modern, graphic impact.

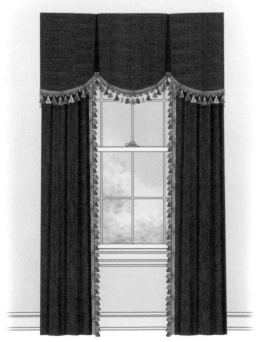

Damask fabric trimmed with bicolor tassel fringe is suited to a quietly formal interior.

A playful animal print trimmed with bright bows makes a charming treatment for a child's room.

valances on knobs or hooks

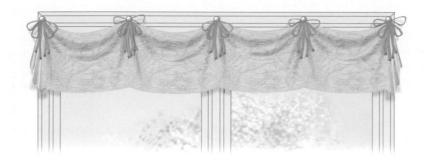

A flat valance tied with double strands of ribbon to pegs on the top molding, on a double window

A flat valance affixed with simple cloth ties to rings in the ceiling

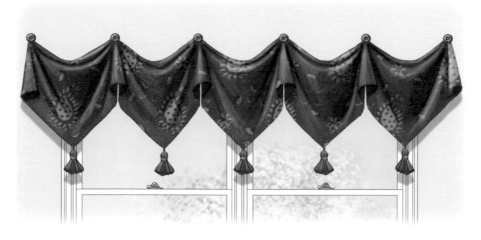

A tassel-trimmed, pointed flat valance draped between knobs on the wall above the window

A draped valance made from a rectangle gathered at the top center and corners and attached to hidden hooks on the wall

A lined valance tied to knobs, allowing the top edge to turn forward in a cuff

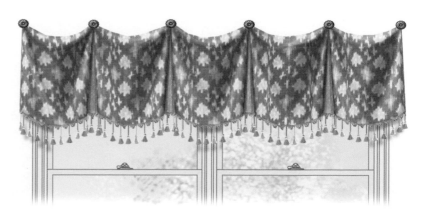

A scalloped valance with complementary inverted pleats and tassel fringe, hung from knobs on the wall above the window

quick, no-sew valance ideas

When you are looking for an easy, do-it-yourself window treatment, a no-sew valance could be just the thing. If you look about with open eyes, you can discover already finished textiles that will make a pretty top treatment or one that's just for fun. Often, all you need to hang it is a curtain rod, some cord and clothespins, or a staple gun.

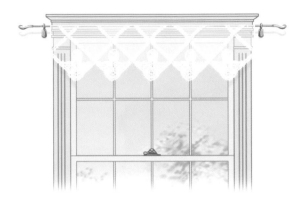

A set of dinner napkins or elegant hankies folded over a curtain pole

Complementary scarves clothespinned to a cord strung across the window top

Two dresser scarves draped over knobs on the top window molding

A set of pennants tied to a curtain pole

Three pairs of cut-off jeans with their belt loops threaded onto a curtain pole

A length of fabric, loosely and randomly twisted and tacked to the window trim

scarf valances

A scarf valance of fabric squares folded diagonally over a pole so the back corners hang lower to show the contrasting lining

A ruffled square hung diagonally to form a scarf valance, with decorative ribbon bows

A scarf valance featuring one large, diagonally hung square flanked by two smaller ones

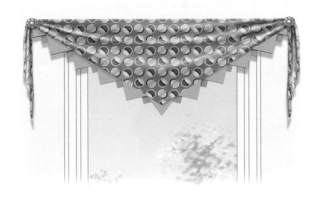

A triangle scarf valance with a sawtooth edging, draped over knobs

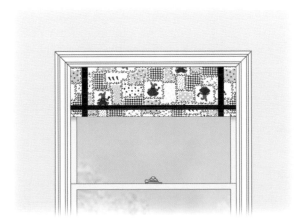

A rectangular scarf valance folded over an inside mounted rod, with ribbon borders crossing at the corners

An elaborate, appliquéd scarf valance folded over a fabric tube that is affixed to decorative knobs on the window molding

stylish ideas for layered valances

If you are looking for greater impact from a valance, consider a style with multiple layers of coordinated fabric. Options range from simple, staggered lengths to playfully juxtaposed hemline shapes. Choose fabric pairings that enhance the effect—this is a good opportunity to showcase stripes or prominent motifs.

A lined flat valance buttoned back to reveal an under layer that matches the lining

A rod pocket valance with a scalloped hemline over a contrasting layer with a straight hemline

A contrasting flat cuff over an inverted pleat valance on a double window, both trimmed with ribbon

Symmetrically overlapped triangles in three sizes and three fabrics, with pompom accents

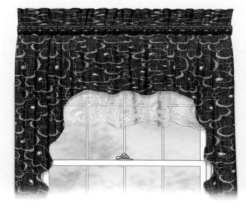
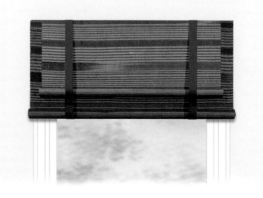

A tapered rod pocket valance in print fabric over a layer of gathered lace

A double stagecoach valance with the top layer narrower and shorter than the under layer

roman valances

A tailed Roman valance with cloth bows beneath the permanent rigging

A skirted, soft Roman valance rigged at the center and sides, on a double window

A crisp Roman valance made from split bamboo and cradled in tasseled tiebacks

A permanently pleated Roman valance with a contrasting border and skirt

A permanently pleated Roman valance with two belt-like supports

A pair of simple, soft Roman valances, inside mounted in a double window

cloud, balloon, and london valances

A barely raised, tailed cloud valance with a small heading

A barely raised, skirted cloud valance with a small heading

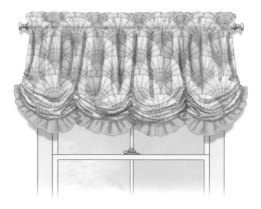

A cloud valance with four poufs and a coordinated ruffle on the lower edge

A grandly proportioned, outside mounted cloud valance with ties cradling the rigging over each mullion on a triple window

A cloud valance with two poufs, a matching ruffle, and large contrasting bows

A cloud valance in an arch window, rigged so the center pouf is higher than the side poufs

A tailed, skirted cloud valance with a heading, on a flat rod

A very large balloon valance, outside mounted on a double window

A soft balloon valance trimmed with multi-loop ribbon bows, decorative cord, and tassels

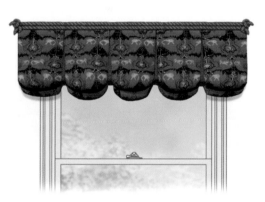

A diminutively proportioned balloon valance with contrasting pleats, topped by two rows of jumbo cord

A simple, plain London valance

An eccentric, tailed and skirted valance pleated at each top corner and trimmed with sawtooth edging

A thoughtfully chosen accent makes a valance look custom-designed and truly finished. Accents needn't be showy or extravagant to be effective—a well-placed, well-proportioned bow or a subtle tassel may add just the perfect touch.

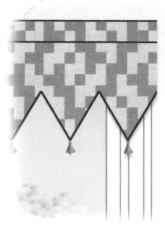

Whimsical bells and contrast trim, highlighting a pointed hemline

A small tassel, enlivening each point on an inverted pleat tab valance

Piping and tassels, accenting a solid border on a patterned valance

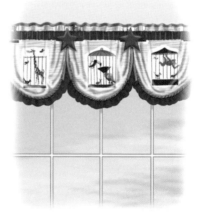

Sprightly stuffed cloth stars, trimming a colorful cloud valance

A tailored bow with long tails, topping an inverted pleat

A lace swag finished with a big pouf knot, softening a flat valance

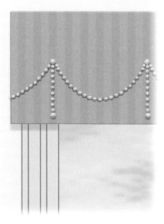

Strings of beads, forming a swag-and-dangle pattern across a flat valance

Bows of ribbon and tasseled cord, decorating a balloon valance

stagecoach valances

An inside mounted stagecoach valance with contrast cloth ties supporting the firm roll

An outside mounted stagecoach valance with large tassels hung in front of the roll from the supporting cords

A stagecoach valance rolled to reveal a coordinated lining, with knotted cloth ties masking the supporting cords

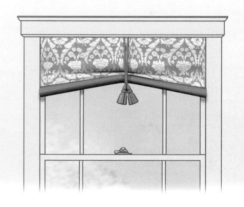

A softly rolled stagecoach valance supported by tasseled decorative cord

A tailed stagecoach valance informally draped up—not rolled—with loops of ribbon

An unusual stagecoach valance with the lower corners buttoned to the top and the fold cradled with ribbon ties

A scarf swag with very short cascades and rosettes masking the swag holders

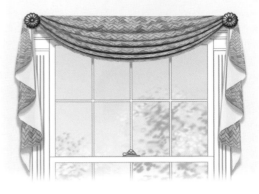

A classic scarf swag with ends folded into neat cascades, draped over knobs

A scarf swag with asymmetric cascades, draped over decorative knobs

A double-drape scarf swag passed through a ring in the center of the pole

A deep scarf swag, lifted at the window center and corners, with the sides falling into soft, informal cascades

Whimsical cloth kitten heads and a center loop of crushed fabric holding a scarf swag

swags and cascades

Rosettes masking the holdbacks supporting a scarf swag on a double window

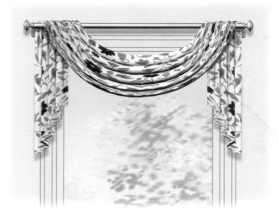

A pleated, deeply draped scarf swag hung over a pole

Three fabrics arranged one above the other on a pole, forming a scarf swag

A generous scarf swag on a double window, draped over a fabric-covered pole

A loosely wrapped scarf swag on a double window, with fancy cockades at each end

An asymmetric, wrapped scarf swag with a large tassel on a cord next to the cascade

stylish ideas for arch window swags

Already curved on one edge, swags are a natural complement to an arch window. Both formal and informal shapes work well—alone, with cascades, and over curtains. There are myriad ways to vary the proportions to accent or downplay the scale of the window.

A large scarf swag arranged in four small drapes and tied into poufs makes a soft frame for a commanding view.

Symmetrically overlapped cutout swags on a curved pole have a traditional demeanor above tied-back panels.

A scarf swag tied up with tassel-trimmed cord adds an understated flourish to an eyebrow window.

A central ruffled swag over matching tied-back side curtains lends charm with its unconventional proportions.

For a formal look, use two swags with a center jabot, side cascades with rosettes, and matching draperies.

scarf swags

A scarf swag arranged so the companion lining is
revealed in the middle swag and cascades

A scarf swag with a contrasting lining and no cascades, draped
over a pole so the swags alternate colors, on a double window

A rectangle of fabric tacked to the window top
and lifted in the middle to form an informal swag

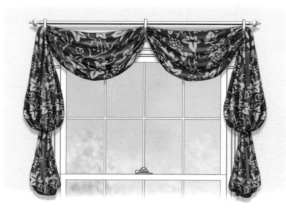

A scarf swag draped through rings on a pole
and rigged to form bishop drape cascades

A scarf swag arranged in swag holders to form a single large drape
on a double window

A scarf swag draped over knobs and tied
into a pouf over each cascade

great tablecloth ideas

Whether you dress a table on occasion or keep it permanently covered, you may wish to choose a tablecloth design that suits an event or season or something that complements your overall décor. Options range from tailored to draped; borders and layers permit you to mix fabrics and colors, and trimmings add an element of fun or luxury.

A square top cloth with a border over a floor-length cloth in another fabric

A very short, scalloped top cloth over a long cloth with a welted hemline

A cloth with a contoured top and two-layer gathered skirt with bound edges

A swagged top cloth with large bows over a matching floor-length cloth

A cloth with a contrasting swagged sash attached around the table top

A long cloth with a deep border under a coordinated square top cloth

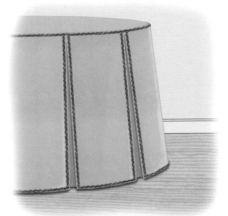

A fitted tablecloth with a braid-trimmed, inverted pleat skirt

A tassel-accented, two-color square cloth, over a fringe-edged cloth

rod pocket swags

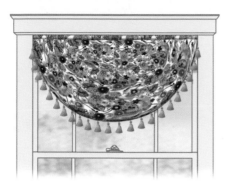

An inside mounted rod pocket swag with
no heading, trimmed with tassel fringe

An outside mounted, ruffled rod pocket
swag with a heading

A rod pocket swag with a heading and
bullion fringe

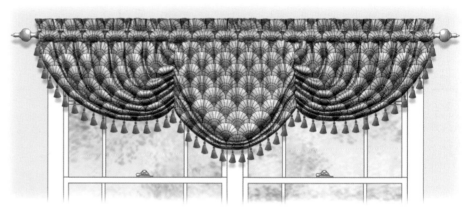

A large rod pocket swag on a double window, divided into
three drapes with vertical shirring and edged with tassel fringe

A large rod pocket swag on a double window, divided with
shirring so the center drape is smaller than the side drapes

Two ruffled rod pocket swags on a single
window, trimmed with rosettes and a
tailed Maltese cross

fabric is key to the look

You might think that a swag belongs only in traditional or high-style decors, but there's nothing inherently fancy about a draped arc of fabric. If you like the soft touch a curved swag brings to a window, you can make this treatment fit any room by choosing a fabric that fits the decorating style. Here's a basic cutout swag made in four different fabrics.

Plain, natural colored linen is at home in tailored, rustic, or minimalist decors.

Use white lace for a pretty, fresh treatment; make it special with tassels hanging from the pole and tips of the cascades.

Pick complementary florals for swag and curtains in an informal traditional décor; add rosette accents and ball fringe for definition.

Jacquard or print fabrics with traditional swirl or arabesque motifs are suited to formal rooms; bullion fringe that matches the lining adds a dressy touch.

swags with cutout tops

A trio of cutout swags on a covered rod, edged with fringe and topped with choux rosettes

A cutout swag with one cascade in front of the pole and one behind it

A double cutout swag with asymmetric cascades, made in two fabrics

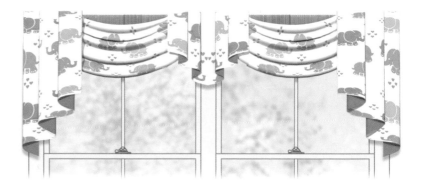

Two cutout swags on a covered rod, topped with cascades and separated by a double jabot

Layered cutout swags, arranged with two large contrasting drapes in front, three small drapes and side cascades in back

A cutout swag and a single cascade, trimmed with a small ruffle

great embellishment ideas

Swag treatments, with all their intersecting arcs and diagonals, are especially suited to embellishments such as prominent tassels and bows. Overlapping areas along swag edges come into focus when set off by braid or fringe. Choose embellishments that match your fabric to give a subtle accent, go for contrast when you want a greater impact.

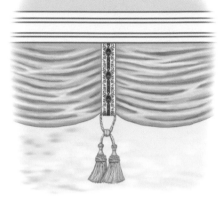

A tassel hanging from a corded button between two swags

Two tassels hanging between fringe-trimmed swags

Two tassels hanging from a ribbon that cradles a vertically shirred swag

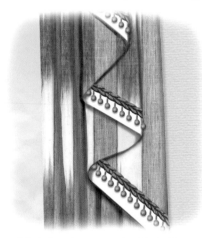

A trio of tassels hanging at the corner of a swag valance

Small tassels hanging from a corded ornament on a skirted shirred swag

A fabric border topped with ball fringe on the top face of a cascade

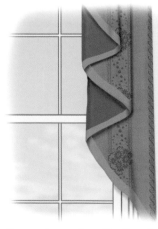

Coordinated tassel fringe along the edge of a cascade

A complementary binding visible on both faces of a cascade

A large, soft, informal multi-loop bow at the corner of a scarf swag

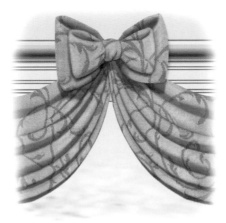

A tailored double bow without tails, placed on the pole between swags

A soft bow with short, pointed tails, between two swags

A large bow with wide, crushed loops and long tails on a ruffled swag

A tailored double bow with tubular tails on a ruffled swag

A crushed double bow with a small ruffle attached to a wide cascade

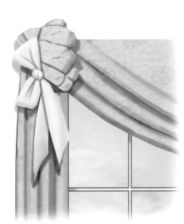

A soft, simple bow tied around a pouf on a scarf swag

Two swirled pieces of fabric at the top of a jabot

swags with closed tops

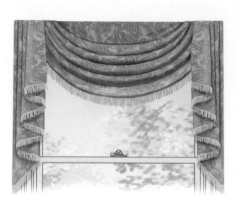

A classic swag under cascades, trimmed with brush fringe and outside mounted

A shallow swag under cascades that have a long top pleat

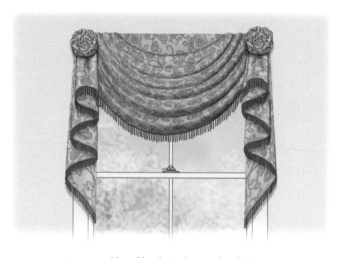

A swag with softly pleated cascades that are topped with choux rosettes

An inside mounted swag under gathered, asymmetric cascades with tall headings

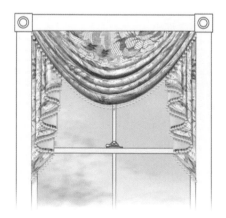

An inside mounted classic swag over cascades, trimmed with ball fringe

An outside mounted classic swag over cascades

A swag mounted on a pole over cascades, trimmed with tassel fringe

A swag that is gathered gently across the top, inside mounted over cascades

A piping-trimmed swag accented with a rosette-centered Maltese cross at each corner

A swag topped with a small cutout swag, accented with spiral rosettes

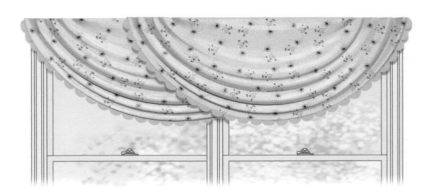

Large, scallop-edged swags outside mounted and overlapped on a double window

An inside mounted swag under cascades, edged with small, coordinated ruffles

great jabot ideas

Jabots are short, soft elements placed between adjacent swags—they hide bulky joins and add a rhythmic balance to longer cascades at the ends of the treatment. Jabots are like short cascades; they have one or two diagonal edges and may be pleated or gathered. On swag valances, the draped sections are separated by a bell-shaped jabot that is similar to a box pleat; these bell jabots are sometimes tapered or gathered at the top.

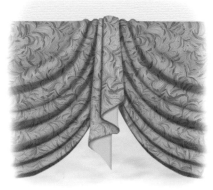

An asymmetric, softly pleated jabot between adjacent swags

A cone shaped jabot, tapered to fit neatly between adjacent swags

A bell jabot on a swag valance

A gathered jabot with a heading, between adjacent swags

A symmetric, crisply pleated double jabot between adjacent swags

A gathered bell jabot on a swag valance

swags with closed tops

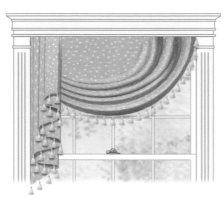

An inside mounted, asymmetrically draped swag under one pleated cascade, trimmed with tassel fringe

An outside mounted swag with one gathered and pleated cascade and complementary but different rosettes

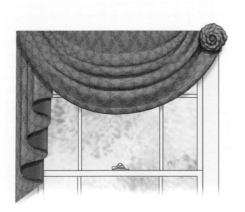

A swag mounted over one cascade, accented with a single spiral rosette

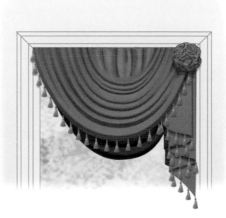

A tassel-fringe-trimmed swag, layered over a second, complementary swag

A curved top swag under pleated cascades with tall headings

A trio of swags over short, wide cascades, outside mounted on a triple window

great cascade ideas

Cascades are the long, hanging elements that frame a single swag or a series of swags; sometimes they are called tails. Cascades may be pleated or gathered and may hang over or under the swag. Small changes in their proportions have great impact on their effect; here are eight that are somewhat out of the ordinary.

A cascade with stacked pleats and a heading

A narrow cascade with a wide top pleat and contrasting lining

A braid-edged cascade with a short inside return and contrasting lining

A flat tail with a curved lower edge, tucked under a swag

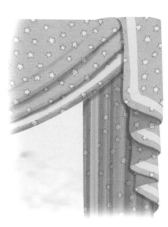

A cascade with an inset, coordinated border and top pleat with curved edge

A wide, gathered cascade edged with tassel fringe

An informal cascade with a pouf heading on a covered rod

A large bow flopped forward over wide tails, standing in for a cascade

swags with closed tops

Three swags symmetrically overlapped on a picture window, over cascades

A small, deep, double swag over cascades, with a third swag centered behind two tassels

An inside mounted, small double swag over cascades, with a large center tassel

An outside mounted double swag over cascades, with a double tassel and coordinated edging

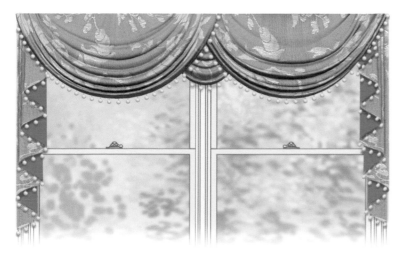

Two large swags, slightly overlapped over a smaller center swag, on a double window

Two swags overlapped on a single window, over cascades with a complementary lining

great rosette ideas

Rosettes, and their Maltese cross and cockade cousins, are the traditional accents for the top corner of a swag. They also work well when strategically placed atop pleats or gathers on other treatments. These dimensional swirls, crushed poufs, and loop assemblies may be fashioned in myriad ways—from simple X-shapes made of looped ribbon to elaborate, flowerlike constructions.

A small Maltese cross with a button center on a pleated valance

A soft Maltese cross with contrasting borders and center button

A soft Maltese cross with small choux rosette center

A Maltese cross with a small spiral rosette center, on a jabot

A Maltese cross with a choux rosette center, topping a large ruffle rosette

A soft Maltese cross with a choux rosette center and tails

A simple spiral rosette masking the holder on a scarf swag

Two fabrics rolled together to make a spiral rosette

A spiral rosette with a center covered button, on a swag with no cascade

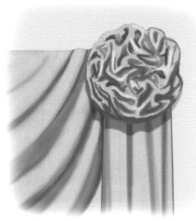

A classic choux rosette, scaled to sit elegantly atop a gathered cascade

A loosely formed choux rosette with a smaller choux rosette center

A simple ruffle rosette with a covered button center

A large, tulle-stuffed ruffle rosette with a small choux rosette center

A choux rosette tucked into the center of a multi-loop bow

A cockade of ribbon loops topped with a ruffle rosette and covered button

A large, fancy cockade with a choux rosette center, hung from a pole

swag valances

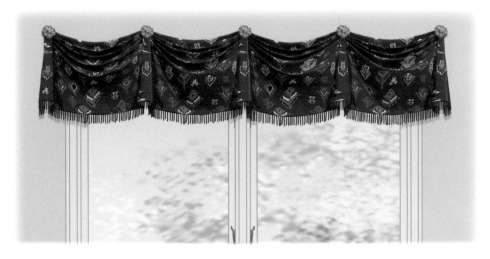

A swag valance outside mounted on a double window, trimmed with fringe and accented with a rosette at the top of each bell jabot

A small swag valance, inside mounted under cascades

A two-layer swag valance with scalloped lower edges and gathered bell jabots

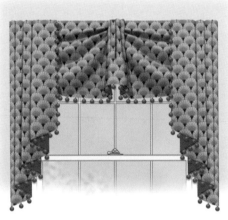

A swag valance with a gathered bell jabot, under cascades and trimmed with ball fringe

A swag valance attached to a band of fabric on a mounting board

A valance with one large swag on each unit of a triple window and a lower border that matches the lining

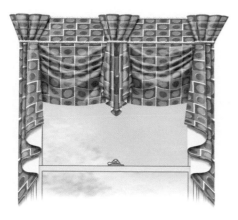

A swag valance attached to a band of fabric, under a jabot and cascades with gathered headings

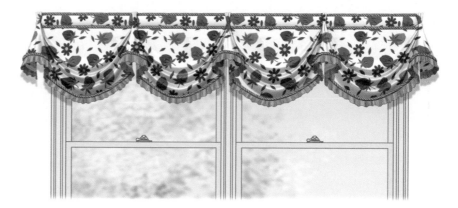

A swag valance with very full pinch pleat jabots, trimmed with a ruffle and cord, and attached to a band of fabric mounted over a double window

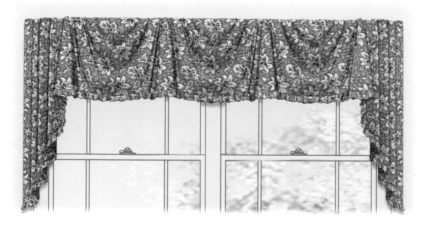

A ruffle-trimmed swag valance with bell jabots at the ends adjacent to cascades, on a double window

A swag valance hung from a small upholstered board, with tassel and ball fringe accents

A ruffle-trimmed swag valance with cascades, accented by double bows with cone tails

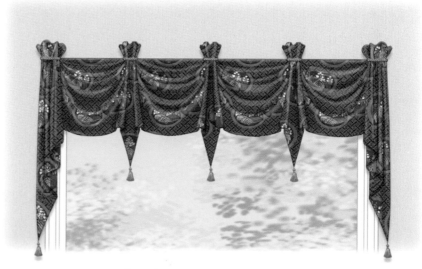

A swag valance featuring tasseled jabots and cascades with gathered headings, on a picture window

swags with a difference

For a window treatment with attitude, consider a swag that's draped in an unconventional manner—with added pleats, an upswept top, or an extra layer. Here are examples from almost simple to extravagantly mannered.

Full and half fan swags, inside mounted and topped with choux rosettes

A cutout swag with the center lifted through a decorative holder, under cascades

A swag lifted and draped over a short pole centered above a window, with double cascades

A swag lifted over a medallion to reveal a contrasting swag, under bow-trimmed cascades

A swag lifted in two places and secured by crushed cockades with choux rosette centers

A double-draped swag releasing into a wide single drape, under cascades with small and large rosettes

vertically shirred swags

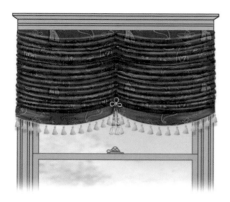

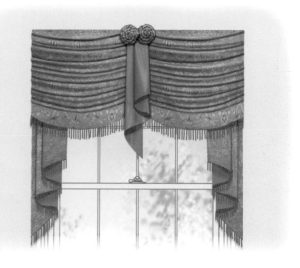

A skirted, vertically shirred swag with tassel fringe and a center tassel ornament, hung from a small cornice

An outside mounted, skirted, vertically shirred swag over cascades, with a simple jabot topped by two rosettes

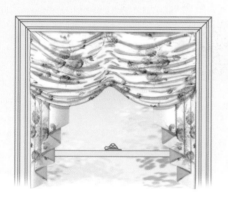

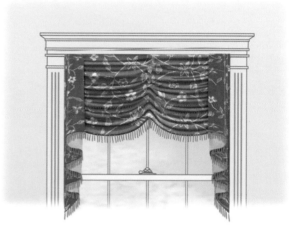

A vertically shirred swag mounted inside the window over wide cascades

A fringe-trimmed, vertically shirred swag mounted under narrow cascades

A swag shirred vertically to form three drapes, over cascades

A swag shirred vertically on the sides only, forming a wide, loose drape

cornices

box cornices

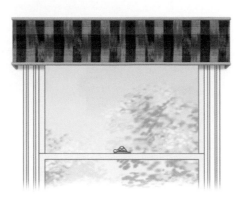

A classic box cornice with piping along the top and bottom edges

A tall box cornice with decorative cord along the top and bottom edges

A cornice with a complementary border inset above the lower edge

A tall cornice decorated with cord threaded through applied ribbon carriers

A cornice overlaid with a wide band of boldly figured fabric

A fabric-covered cornice with applied moldings and a railing for display of small objects

A very short cornice covered in the same border fabric used to decorate the roller shade

A short cornice upholstered in three padded sections, over matching panels

A tall cornice decorated with contrasting cord applied in spiraled rounds and with cord swags and tassels

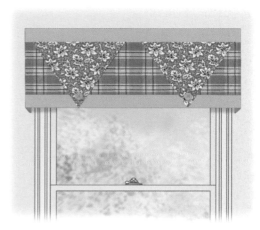

A tall cornice with contrasting borders and triangular overlays buttoned at the tips

A cornice covered with neatly pleated fabric secured with cord set in from the top and bottom edges

An upholstered cornice with extra padding under the top and bottom contrast borders

great embellishment ideas

Choose embellishment materials that complement the cornice covering and use them to relieve a plain, flat expanse or enhance an exaggerated or eccentric shape. Flat trimmings like ribbon provide graphic detail; three-dimensional ones like swags and tassels soften boxy shapes.

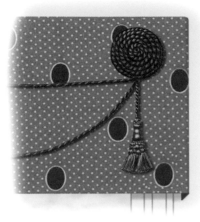

An appliqué of coiled cord atop a tassel and swagged cords

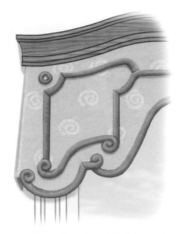

Ribbon gathered and swirled to make a formal design on a cornice skirt

Wide ribbon gathered along inside curves to follow a complex outline

A wood appliqué on a wood cornice with moldings

Cord and button trim above tassels on a deeply notched cornice skirt

A stuffed, quilted motif worked on the fabric covering a cornice

An edging of matching, fabric-covered cord on an upholstered cornice

A jabot with a choux rosette and tassel on a swag-embellished cornice

cornices with simple shapes

A cornice cut at the bottom to echo the shape of an eyebrow window

A cornice with an angled notch cutout on the lower edge

A wide cornice with a small arch cutout on a double window, with cord along the lower edge

A cornice with a gentle arch cut from side to side across the lower edge

A cornice with a peaked curve cut into the lower edge, trimmed with fringe

A cornice with a gentle downward curve centered on the lower edge

scalloped cornices

A cornice with end scallops on the lower edge, trimmed with tassel fringe

A cornice with half scallops flanking a large center scallop on the lower edge, trimmed with cord

A cornice with small scallops flanking a large scallop on the lower edge, trimmed with cord

A cornice with small scallops across the center and deeper half scallops at the ends

A cornice with a scallop and point lower edge, trimmed with braid

A scallop and point cornice on a double window, trimmed with two adjacent covered cords

A scallop and point cornice with the sides longer than the center, trimmed with fringe

A scallop and point cornice with longer sides and two scallops in the center

A scallop and point cornice with longer sides and a center point

A tall cornice cut with an arch and point on each side of a large center scallop

A scallop and point cornice on a double window, featuring asymmetric points

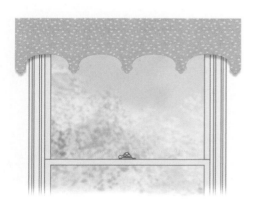

A short, uniquely shaped, reversed scallop cornice

cornices with complex shapes

A cornice with unusual arch cutouts, a tabbed center, and very long sides, trimmed with fringe

An intricate cornice with extended, rounded sides, outlined with ribbon

A cornice with flared, pointed sides and scallop-edged cutout

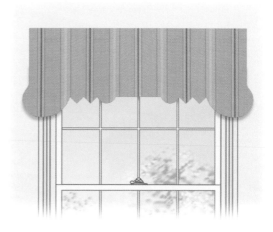

A tall cornice with slightly extended, rounded sides and scallops and double points on the lower edge

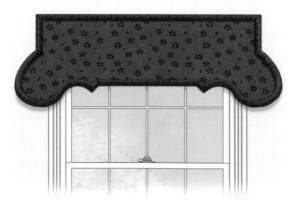

A ribbon-outlined cornice with boldly extended, rounded sides and points on the lower edge

An elaborate cornice with flared sides and a peaked top, draped with decorative cord

swag and rosette trimmed cornices

A plain box cornice draped with a fringed swag made of complementary fabric

A box cornice on a double window, draped with overlapping swags and edged with decorative cord

A tall cornice with a scallop and point edge and applied contrast swags, jabots, rosettes, and tassels

A boldly scalloped cornice with a center tab, trimmed with an applied swag, rosettes, and tassel fringe

A scalloped cornice with swags topped by a double jabot and cascades

A scallop and notch cornice decorated with rosettes, applied fans of gathered fabric, and fringe

plain and fancy surface treatments

For the do-it-yourself decorator, readymade cornices are available in a variety of profiles. There are rigid foam models with crevices for tuck-in upholstery and wood ones ready to finish with paint or stain. Here are some finishing ideas.

Three fabrics tucked into a foam cornice form with a capital profile

One plain and one border-print fabric tucked into a foam cornice form with square-edge top and bottom moldings

Two fabrics tucked into a foam cornice form with a gently rounded middle section

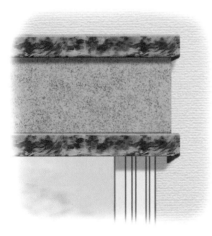

A sponge-painted wood cornice with faux tortoise-shell moldings

A wood cornice painted in faux malachite, with solid color moldings

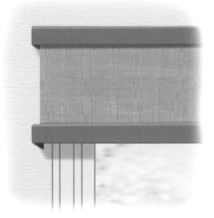

A wood cornice painted with a moiré combing technique

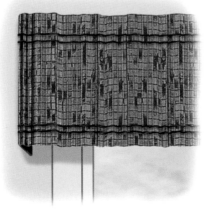

Split bamboo placemats glued to the surface of a plain cornice

A cornice covered in cork for easy picture display

wood cornices

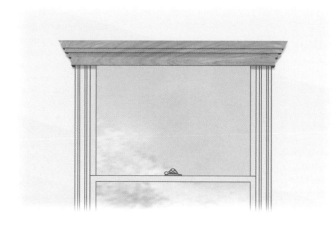

A simple wood cornice with crown molding

A wood cornice decorated with a wood appliqué, painted to show off the moldings

A simple wood cornice decorated with metal holdback faceplates

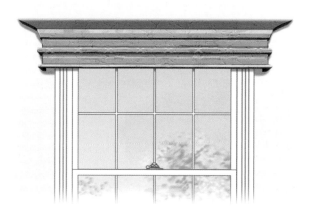

An elaborate wood cornice with grand moldings and gilt accents

A wood cornice embossed with silver-gilt three-dimensional diamonds

A scallop and point wood cornice decorated with incised carving and chunky wood cutouts, on a double window

awning cornices have bold allure

An awning cornice slopes away from the wall to make a canopy over the window. These cornices may have a flat surface, often with open sides, or they may be rounded. The more complex the shape and fabrication of an awning cornice, the more dramatic its effect.

Painted knobs at the top and tassels at the hem jazz up a simple awning cornice with a boldly pointed lower edge.

A frame with finials makes a decorative support for a scalloped awning cornice with tassel-fringe trim.

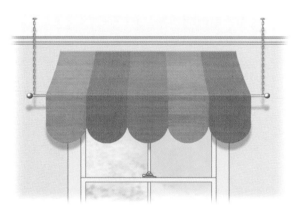

A pole supported by chains accents the playful effect of a multi-color, striped and scalloped awning cornice.

A tailored dome cornice gets a bold finish from coordinating trim that outlines each section.

Ruffles, a scalloped skirt, and a big bow at the top enhance the fanciful effect of a tent cornice.

A deep, gently scalloped skirt, trimmed with ball fringe, makes a graceful finish for a tent cornice.

skirted cornices

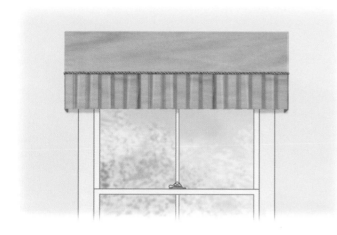

A tall cornice with a skirt of small, regular pleats

A cornice with a ruffled skirt that features a generous sawtooth edge

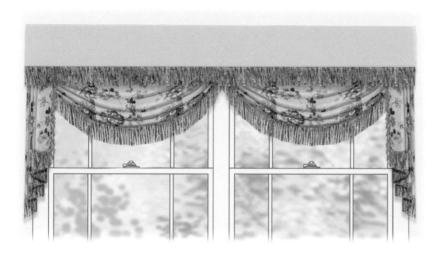

A fringed cornice skirted with coordinating fringed swags and cascades, on a double window

A grand wood cornice with a fringe-trimmed, inverted pleat skirt

A curved top cornice with painted wood molding and an ornate, ribbon-embossed skirt

An upholstered cornice with a deeply notched skirt trimmed with tassels

blinds

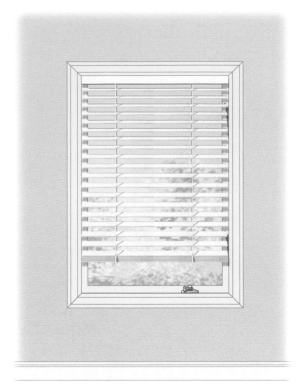

A horizontal blind with exposed rigging cords, mounted inside the window

A horizontal blind with cloth ladder tape over the rigging cords, mounted outside the window

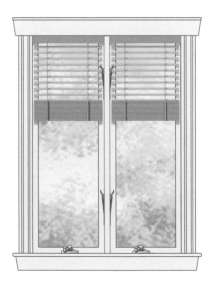

A pair of mini-blinds, inside mounted on casement windows

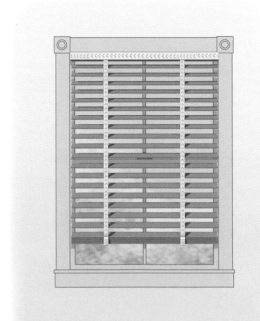

A blind with decorative cloth tape over the rigging and on the valance

A blind with the slats divided into four
contrasting bands of color

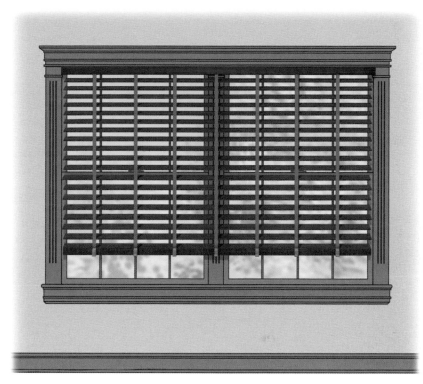

A single, wide blind on a double window

Two floor-length blinds, mounted under a single valance
above a double door

A mini-blind, sash-mounted on a door

vertical blinds

A pair of vertical blinds, sash-mounted on double doors

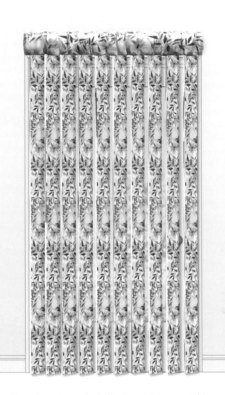

Floor-length vertical blinds under a matching, fabric-covered cornice, on a single door

Apron-length, outside mounted vertical blinds

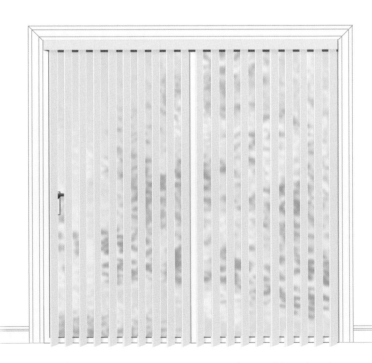

Floor-length vertical blinds, inside mounted on a sliding glass door

blinds under draperies and curtains

A classic horizontal blind under pleated draperies

A wood blind under shirred draperies on a floor-length window

A blind under rod pocket curtains

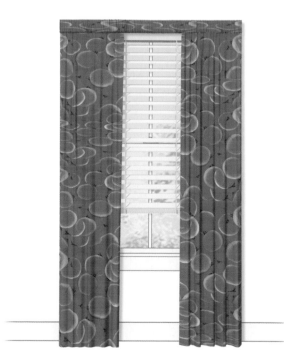

A blind under rod pocket curtains separated by a rod sleeve

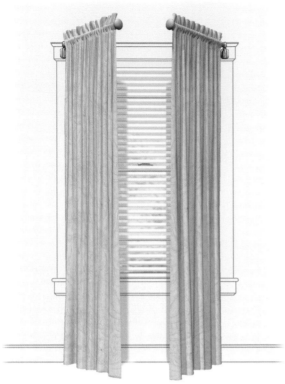

An inside mounted blind under swing-out rod pocket curtains

A blind under a wood cornice and curtains with double-drape rigging

A pair of blinds under tabbed curtains that are folded in tiebacks so that the complementary lining is revealed

A blind under cuffed curtains with tasseled tiebacks

blinds under valances

A blind inside mounted under a small, inside mounted, painted wood valance

A blind under a pleated valance with handkerchief points

A mini-blind under a tabbed valance

A blind under a stagecoach valance

blinds under valances

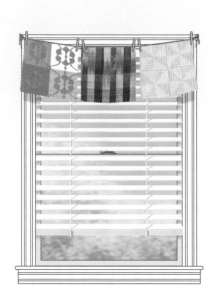

A blind under a valance of assorted, colorful scarves or napkins

A mini-blind under a ruffle-trimmed, triangle scarf valance

A pair of blinds under a single, pleated and scalloped valance on a double window

A blind under a pouf valance

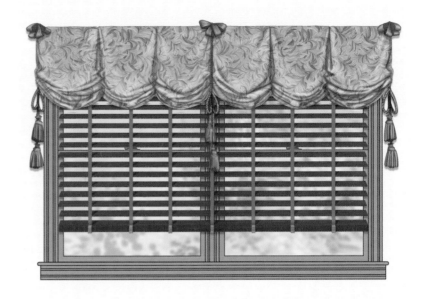

A blind under a tailed rod pocket valance with a tied, ribbon accent

A single, wide blind on a double window under an elegant, tassel-and-bow accented balloon valance

A blind under a ruffled cloud valance trimmed with large bows

A mini-blind under a tailed cloud valance, both sash-mounted on a door

blinds under swags

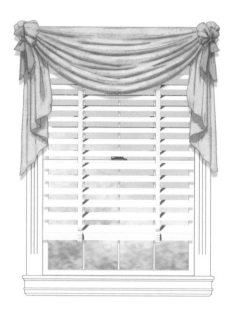

A horizontal blind under a scarf swag with small poufs secured by soft bows

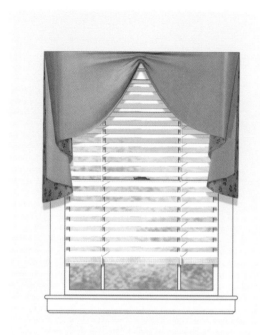

A blind under an informal scarf swag

A vertical blind, inside mounted under a scarf swag draped over holdback knobs

A blind under a double-draped scarf swag

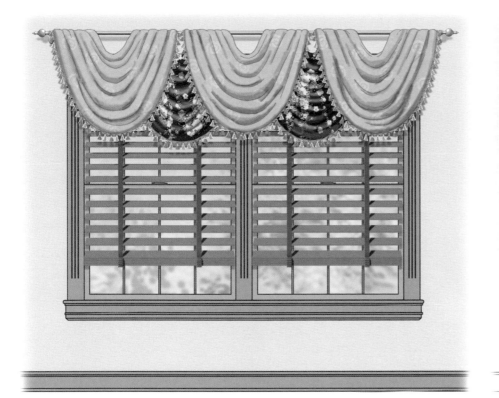

A pair of blinds under a deeply draped scarf swag with a contrasting lining, on a double window

A blind under an asymmetric, cutout double swag

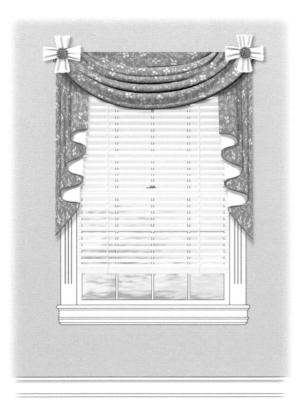

A mini-blind under a classic swag and cascades with Maltese cross accents

A pair of blinds under cutout swags topped with cascades and a center jabot, on a covered rod

blinds under swags

A blind under a swag with a cascade and rosette on opposite corners

A wood blind under a double swag with cascades and a large tassel accent

A mini-blind under pouf-topped, sheer cascades on a sleeve-covered rod

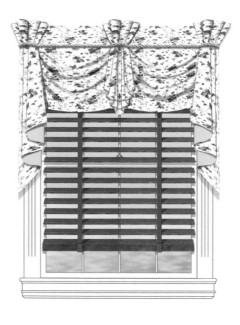

A wood blind under a swag valance with cascades and a heading

blinds under cornices

A blind with contrasting cloth ladder tapes, inside mounted under a simple box cornice

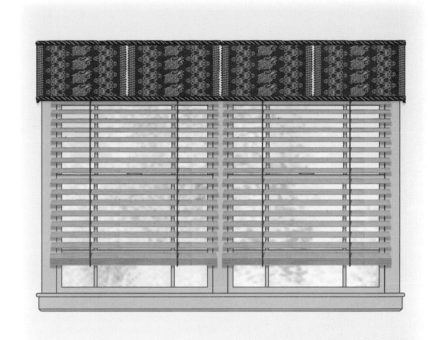

A pair of wood blinds outside mounted under a single box cornice

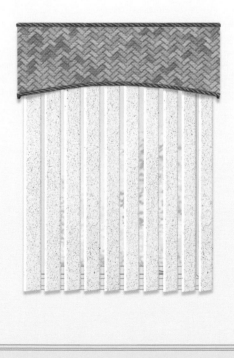

A vertical blind, outside mounted under a cornice with a gently arched lower edge

A wood blind under a cornice with a wide notch cutout on the lower edge

blinds under cornices

A blind under a boldly scalloped cornice

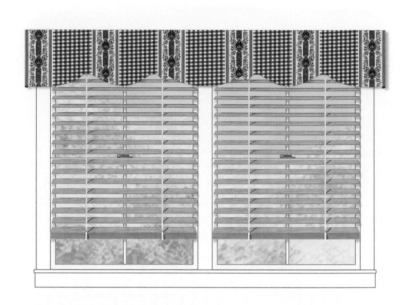

A pair of blinds inside mounted under a single scallop and point cornice

An outside mounted blind under a cornice with flared sides

A mini-blind outside mounted under a scalloped awning cornice

blinds under curtains and top treatments

A blind under a simple, flat valance and curtains

A blind under a scalloped flat valance and curtains

A blind with contrasting cloth ladder tapes,
under a rod pocket valance and short curtains

A blind under a tapered rod pocket
valance and curtains with tasseled tiebacks

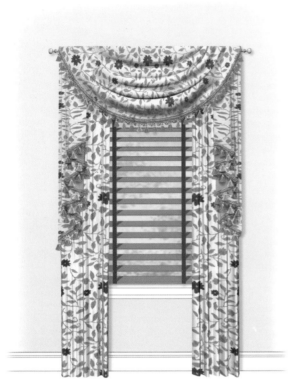

A blind under a swag, cascades, and
curtains mounted on a pole

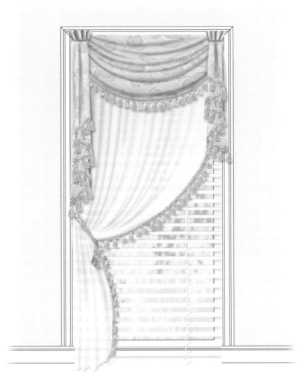

A formal arrangement of a swag, single
sheer curtain, and floor-length blind

A single, wide blind under a swag valance and curtains on
a double window

A mini-blind under a vertically shirred swag,
cascades, and curtains draped over holdbacks

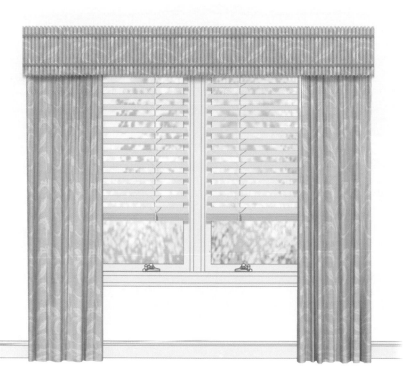

A pair of blinds under curtains and a single cornice covered with finely pleated fabric, on a double window

A mini-blind under a grand wood cornice and simple curtains with tiebacks

A blind under a scallop and point cornice and matching curtains

A floor-length blind under an ornate cornice and plain curtains

shutters and screens

A single louvered shutter on a single window

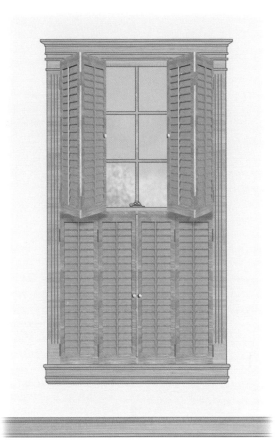

Two pairs of bi-fold louvered shutters on a tall single window

Two pairs of louvered shutters of unequal heights on a single window

A single bi-fold louvered shutter

A pair of louvered shutters on a double window

A single louvered shutter on a door

A bi-fold louvered shutter on a door

Sliding bypass shutters on a sliding double door

panel shutters

A single, raised-panel shutter on a single window

A pair of bi-fold panel shutters on a single window

A pair of combination louver-and-board shutters on a single window

Two pairs of panel shutters on a tall single window

A pair of bi-fold shutters, each section featuring two square panels separated by two long panels

A pair of bi-fold shutters, each section divided into four equal panels

A pair of bi-fold shutters, each section divided with alternating square and rectangular panels

A pair of bi-fold shutters on a floor-length window, each section divided into four unequal panels

fabric shutters are unique and lightweight

Fabric inserts make it possible to coordinate shutters with other textiles in a room. They offer a tailored window covering that's a bit softer than wood and, depending on the fabric chosen, may look either modern or traditional. They're a good choice for interior windows and cabinet and closet doors too.

Solid color, opaque fabric panels are neat and trim.

A panel featuring a large-print fabric has picture-like impact.

Sheer fabric panels soften unenticing views without blocking light.

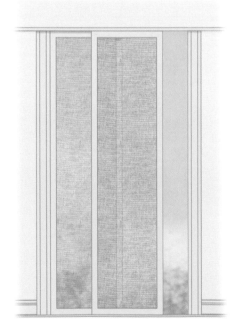

Translucent linen sliding panels create a graphic stripe when overlapped.

A prominent, figured-stripe fabric is a handsome architectural complement.

A panel filled with a whimsical print fabric adds fun to a youngster's room.

shutters under draperies and curtains

Louvered shutters under shirred draperies with
a coordinated lining and holdbacks

Louvered shutters under rod pocket curtains
separated by a rod sleeve

Bi-fold panel shutters under inside-mounted,
short, shirred draperies

Louvered shutters under double-layer curtains
on rings

shutters under valances

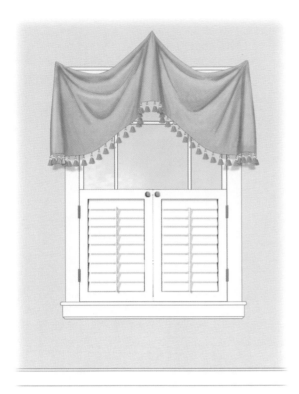

Louvered shutters on the lower half of a window, below a scarf valance with a lifted center

Louvered shutters under a cuffed scarf valance that is tied to knobs

Louvered shutters under a tapered rod pocket valance

Three-quarter-height louvered shutters under a skirted cloud valance rigged so the hemline is level

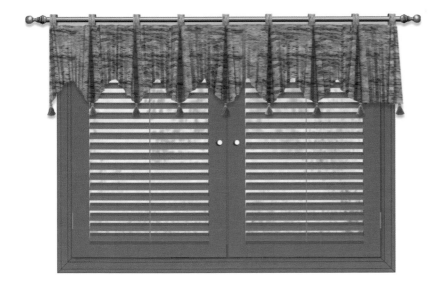

Louvered shutters in a double window under a pleated tab valance with pointed hem

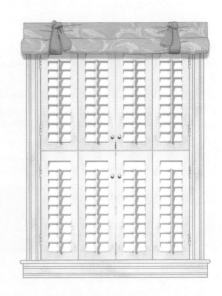

Two pairs of bi-fold louvered shutters under a short stagecoach valance

Louvered shutters under a scalloped, inverted pleat valance

Bi-fold louvered shutters on a double window under a cuffed, pleated valance

shutters under swags

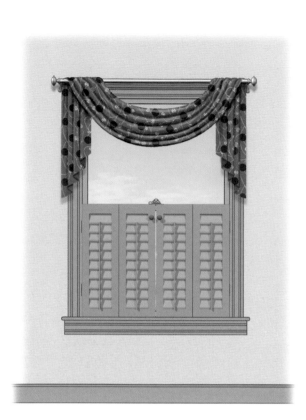

Bi-fold louvered shutters on the lower half of a window, under a scarf swag

Rectangular louvered shutters on an arch window under a floor-length scarf swag with small poufs

Louvered shutters under overlapping, closed-top swags with cascades

Louvered shutters on a double window under a wrapped scarf swag with fancy cockade accents

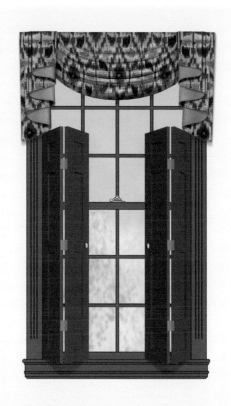

Three-quarter-height bi-fold panel shutters under a swag and cascades on a tall window

Louvered shutters under a swag and cascades

Louvered shutters on the lower half of a window, below an inside mounted triple swag and cascades

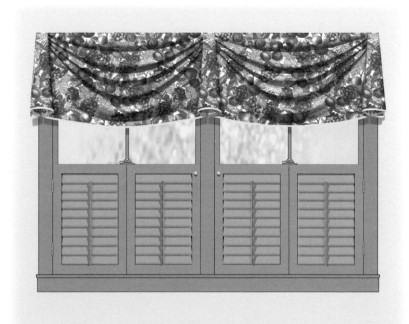

Bi-fold louvered shutters on the lower half of a double window, below a swag valance

decorative shutter finishing ideas

Use multiple paint colors to break up shutter surfaces, or go for a decorative or faux-finishing technique that ties to your overall decorating style. Here are just a few options for both louvered and panel shutters.

Louvered sections painted to contrast with the frame and window moldings

A light-hearted, spatter-paint finish on shutters and window moldings

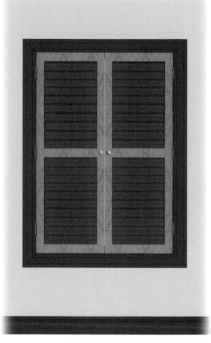

Louvered sections, frames, and window moldings—each finished with a different wood stain

A pickled and then distressed finish on shutters and window moldings

Stenciled motifs centered on vivid, outlined panels

Panels colorfully painted with a wood-graining roller

shutters under cornices

A louvered shutter under an upholstered cornice with buttoned, triangular overlays

Bi-fold panel shutters on the lower half of a window, below a reversing scallop cornice

Bi-fold panel shutters under a deep cornice with a double-swag skirt and cascades

Louvered shutters on the lower half of a window, below an awning cornice

shutters under curtains with top treatments

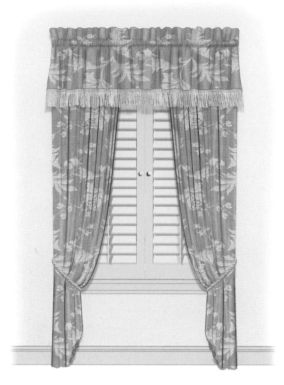

Louvered shutters under a fringe-trimmed rod pocket valance and curtains

A louvered shutter under tab curtains separated by a short tab valance

Bi-fold louvered shutters on the lower half of a double window, under two triangle scarf valances with curtains

Louvered shutters on the lower half of a tall window, under a cloud valance and curtains

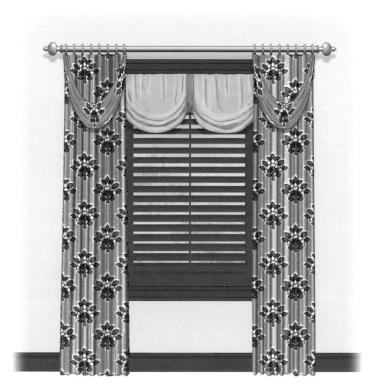

A louvered shutter under an informal stagecoach valance and ring curtains with shawl swags

Bi-fold panel shutters under a cutout swag with cascades and curtains

Louvered shutters in an eyebrow window under a notched cornice and curtains

Bi-fold louvered shutters under a skirted wood cornice with curtains

shutter options for special windows

Shutters can be made to fit nearly any window shape, or any configuration of multiple units in a window wall. You can customize not only the overall shape, but also the number of shutter sections to go on each window. Windows that have an arched pane set inside a square sash (found in some period homes) look at first glance as if they require specially shaped shutters, but they don't.

A pair of louvered shutters shaped to an arch window

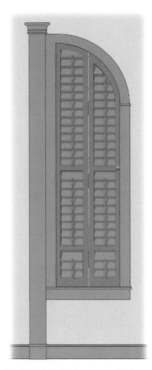

A single bi-fold louvered shutter shaped to a half-arch window

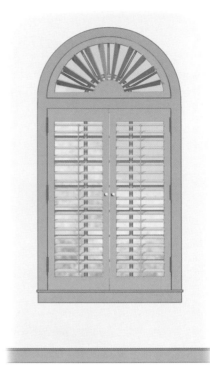

Louvered shutters with a separate fan top in an arch window

A single louvered shutter shaped to an eyebrow window

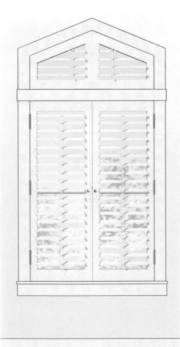

Two pairs of louvered shutters fitted to a pointed arch window

Rectangular shutters on a window with an arched pane in a square sash

sliding shoji screens

A sliding shoji screen on a single window

Two bypass sliding shoji screens on a double window

A sliding shoji screen on a floor-length window

Two bypass sliding shoji screens on a double sliding door

bed furnishings

A very simple, gathered curtain fixed to the top frame at the head of the bed

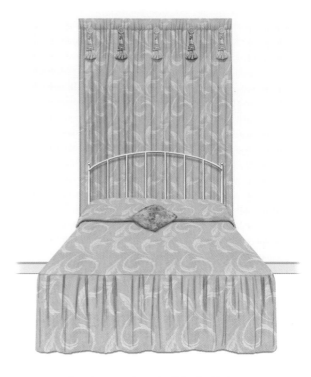

A rod pocket curtain embellished with large tassels, mounted on the wall behind the bed

An inverted pleat curtain mounted on the wall and extending on brackets to form a small enclosure

A flat panel hung by tabs from a simple pole mounted on the wall behind the bed

four-poster beds with curtains

Delicate lace rod pocket curtains hung at the head corners of the bed frame

Rod pocket curtains hung at each corner of the bed frame and extending behind the head

Rod pocket curtains with headings and fringe on the vertical edges, hung at each corner of the bed frame

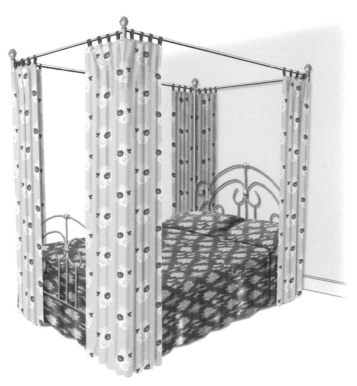

Tab curtains hung at each corner of the bed frame

no-fuss bed hangings

With a bit of ingenuity (and even without a four-poster bed), you can create charming, informal bed hangings. Here are some clever ideas that require little or no sewing.

Sheer fabric draped over two ceiling-hung rods

Fabric draped over the frame and tied to opposite corners

Two lengths of fabric draped crosswise over the bed frame

A long piece of fabric wrapped in swags over the bed frame

A flat canopy and panels simply tied to the bed frame

A ceiling-hung track with panels on shower curtain rings

four-poster beds with top treatments

A double-arch canopy with a short, ruffled valance

A knotted or crocheted lace canopy with a matching, flat, scalloped valance

A rod-pocket valance with a small heading

An arch canopy with a double-ruffle valance, accented with large bows

great pillow ideas

Accent pillows make a bed look well-dressed. Whether you're covering throw pillows, big European squares, small neck rolls, or substantial bolsters, you may use fabrics that match the rest of your bed furnishings or provide a contrasting touch. Here are some ideas that work in a variety of sizes.

A pillowcase with an extending button-through cuff

A simple sham with a centered, three-button placket

A sham with a flange on three sides and a tied closure on the fourth side

A sham made of three fabrics, with an off-center button placket

An envelope pillow cover with bound edges and tie fastenings

An envelope sham with a flange on three sides and a button flap

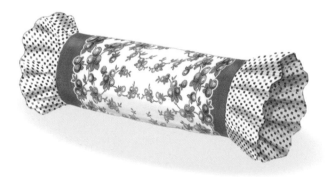

A cylindrical bolster cover with a ruffle at each end

A rectangular bolster with a giftwrap-style cover secured with a decorative frog

Two end covers slipped over a pillow and tied together

A round pillow cover with an applied ruffle with bound edges

A tailored sham with a scalloped flange with bound edges

A boxed pillow cover with shirred sides and a ruffle around the bottom

A printed-square pillow cover trimmed with scalloped fringe

A rectangular sham with a frog closure and lace overlays at the ends

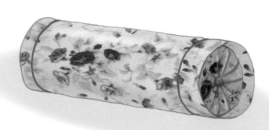

A cylindrical bolster cover with a flange at each end

A pillow cover with a flange scalloped in scale with the checked fabric

four-poster beds with curtains and top treatments

A simple, flat valance wrapped around the outside of the bed frame and over curtains at each corner

A scalloped flat valance, over curtains that extend across the bed head and are tied back at the sides

A box-pleat valance attached to the bed frame and topped with a molding, over corner curtains

A gathered valance with a heading, over curtains that extend across the bed head and are tied back at the sides

A gathered valance over curtains that are tied back around each bed post

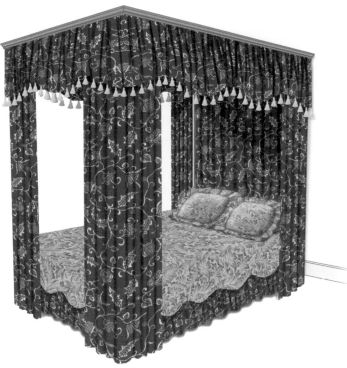

A deep, gathered valance attached to the bed frame and topped with a molding, over bed-head and corner curtains

An arch canopy with a head curtain, side swags, and long corner cascades, trimmed with ball fringe and large tassels

A swag valance with cascades over corner curtains

Any basic curtain design—rod pocket, tab, tie, or eyelet top—can be used on a four-poster bed. To create your preferred look, choose fabric in a color and style that fits the mood you desire; then incorporate details such as a contrasting lining or borders, tiebacks, and fringe or another trim.

Lightweight, pastel fabric is simple and pretty; contrasting ribbons tied in delicate bows dress it up without fuss.

Vivid colors and a fun, floral lining create a cheery spot in which to rise and shine.

A richly hued paisley print paired with a contrasting, deep bottom border complements a tailored décor.

An allover floral pattern dressed up with a fringe-trimmed vertical border gives a classic look.

bed-head canopies

A small canopy with a flat valance between bell jabots, mounted over a panel that extends around the bed head

A painted, wood cornice with a gathered ceiling drape and hanging panels across the bed head and at the sides

A small pleated canopy with a pointed hem, coordinated border, and large tassels, mounted over gathered panels

A wrought-iron canopy frame with a gathered cover that extends to form a valance and bed-head curtain

great ottoman ideas

Nothing beats an ottoman for casual sitting or propping up slippered feet. Whether you choose upholstery or a slipcover to dress an ottoman, there are myriad options that can be coordinated with your window treatments. Here are just a few to get you thinking.

A lined fabric square with the corners folded up and secured by tassels

A tailored cover decorated with large appliqués and Maltese crosses

A plump, upholstered ottoman with a skirt pleated to match the top sections

A tufted, upholstered ottoman with braid trim and a luxurious fringe skirt

A tufted, upholstered ottoman with a gathered skirt topped with cord

A cover with a gathered skirt with cord, braid, and long fringe

A cover with a piped, yoked top and gathered skirt with an applied ruffle

A cover with a piped, yoked top, gathered skirt, and tiered ruffles

bed-head canopies

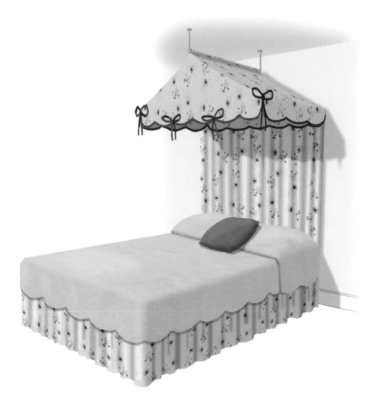

A scalloped tent canopy suspended from the ceiling, with a curtain gathered across the bed head

A swagged canopy fixed to a ceiling-mounted cornice, over a curtain gathered across the bed head and at the sides

A small canopy with a gathered valance with a heading, over a curtain gathered across the bed head and at the sides

An alcove hung with curtains that are tied back on each side of the bed, similar in effect to a canopy

great coverlet, duvet, and bed-skirt combinations

Coordinated bed coverings make a bedroom look composed and inviting. The style of your bed itself may influence the type of coverings you choose, as will your preference for readymade or sewn-to-order bed fashions. Choose linens that work with the mix.

A matching coverlet and gathered bed skirt, both with tassel fringe

A short coverlet with tiny scallops on the edge, over a long, pleated skirt

A coverlet edged with jumbo cord, over a gathered lace skirt

A fringe-trimmed coverlet over a skirt with widely spaced box pleats

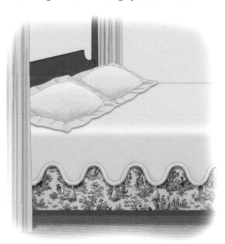

A coverlet with a reversing scallop hemline, over a covered box spring

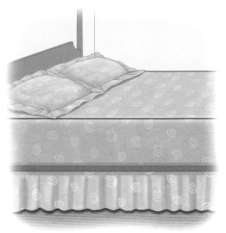

A coverlet with contrasting piping and binding, over a matching skirt

A fitted comforter with a folded throw, over a covered box spring

A neatly wrapped mattress on a platform with a tailored, skirted cover

An unevenly scalloped coverlet over a covered, fringe-trimmed box spring

A coverlet with contrasting trim, gathered skirt, and folded comforter

A coverlet with large scallops on the edge, gathered skirt, and folded quilt

A bedspread with an attached gathered skirt with a deep border

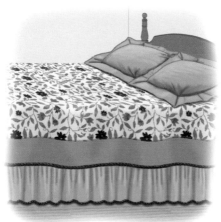

A print-covered duvet, over a coordinated coverlet and skirt

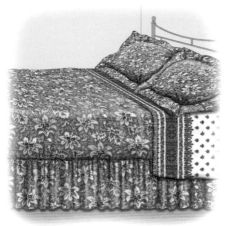

A pretty sheet folded over a duvet cover with an attached, deep ruffle

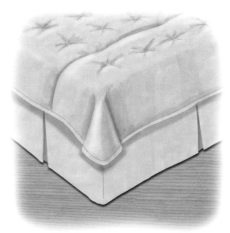

A button-tufted comforter and matching kick-pleat skirt

A fitted mattress cover with a folded throw, over a lapped sectional skirt

use cord and braid to accent and outline

To break up the wide expanse of bed coverings, introduce a linear detail with cord, braid, or binding. If all the fabric in an ensemble is the same color, these trimmings help to separate the layers; where the fabrics differ, the trims enhance the overall effect.

Contrasting cord, outlining a coverlet and the shirred border on a bed skirt

Contrasting binding and matching cord, framing a bedspread perimeter

Two unequal flanges, pleated at the corners, accenting a duvet edge

Solid color trims along the sides and button band on a one-fabric duvet

Binding accenting a coordinated envelope flap and button band

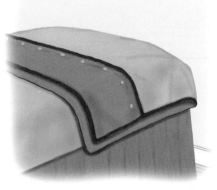

Bright, contrasting binding on a plain two-color duvet

A duvet trimmed with binding and ties that match a bed skirt below

A coordinated binding that enhances both fabrics on a two-sided duvet

bed crowns

A simple, scallop-edged curtain attached to ring suspended invisibly from the ceiling

lab curtains hung on a semicircular, wrought-iron wall bracket and draped to each side of the bed

A gathered panel with a heading and a coordinated lining, on a semicircular, wall-mounted frame

Two panels gathered onto a wall-mounted, half-round crown and draped to each side of the bed

bed crowns

A panel with a contrasting lining, gathered onto a storybook crown suspended invisibly from the ceiling over a crib

A flat-tab valance and gathered curtains fixed to a wall-mounted, half-round crown

A shirred valance with a shaped hemline over gathered panels with a complementary lining, fixed to a half-oval frame

A rod pocket valance with a contrasting scalloped border over curtains, on a small semicircular frame

A shirred, ruffle-trimmed valance over curtains with a complementary lining, on a semicircular frame

A cloud shade valance over curtains, both trimmed with tassel fringe, on a semicircular frame

Swags and cascades over side curtains, hung from a generously sized, upholstered, semicircular frame

Simple swags topped with rosettes over side curtains, hung from a large, painted, semicircular wood frame

start with a design

Successful window treatments depend upon good planning. You might think your first step should be to measure your window; but, in truth, until you have decided upon the design of your curtain, shade, valance, or other treatment, you won't know which measurements to take or where to take them. So first off, choose the kind of window treatment you want, decide how you'll mount it so you'll know the hardware requirements, and then start to think about the style of the fabric and any visible hardware.

decide on inside or outside mount

Window treatments can hang inside or outside the window frame. Those that hang inside the frame leave the window molding uncovered so it remains part of the décor and are generally no longer than the windowsill. Curtains and draperies that hang outside the window frame usually conceal the window molding and may be whatever length you like. Outside mounted treatments can be sized and positioned to visually alter or disguise the proportions of the window; this is especially true of treatments that combine a top component—a cornice or swag, for instance—with hanging panels.

INSIDE MOUNTS. Almost any curtain, valance, shade, or swag design can be mounted inside the window, affixed usually to a rod suspended between the sides of the recess or to a board screwed to the top of the recess. Just bear in mind, that, when pulled open, inside mounted curtains can't be drawn completely off the glass; instead, they'll stack against sides of the window recess. Treatments mounted inside the window do not require fabric at the sides to return to the wall.

OUTSIDE MOUNTS. Depending on your design, you can hang an outside mounted treatment from a traverse rod, a curtain rod or pole with or without decorative finials, or a mounting board; cornices attach directly to the wall. Treatments hung on poles with finials do not make a return to the wall on their outside edges. Except for blinds, roll-up shades, and Roman shades, treatments hung on boards, traverse rods, or U-shaped rods do return to the wall, and an allowance for this must be figured into the fabric requirements. Outside mounted curtains and draperies may be designed so they pull open to one side or both sides; they may be secured with tiebacks or holdbacks if desired.

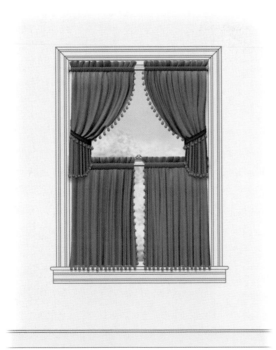

Two pairs of inside mounted café curtains, with tiebacks holding the top pair open

Curtains on a pole with finials, outside mounted at the top of the window molding, with one side held open in a tieback

measure your window the right way

To estimate the amount of fabric you need for a window treatment or to order window fashions from a mail-order source, you must first measure your window. The best approach, the one used by professionals, is to work from the dimensions of the window itself and not from the hardware. Turn to "top treatment proportions" on page 194 to learn some conventions for lengths of top treatments. If you are having your treatments custom-made, ask the workroom to do the measuring; if ordering from a catalog, measure as instructed.

For accuracy, use a steel tape measure and ask someone to help you. Refer to the drawing at left.

For inside mounted treatments, measure the width of the opening (A) and the length (B).

For outside mounted treatments, you must first determine the amount of wall that will be covered by your treatment. Then measure the width of the opening (A) and the length (B), the extension to the left (C) and right (D) of the opening, and the distance above (E) and below (F) it.

- The total of these width measurements is part of the fullness ratio used to determine fabric requirements for curtains, draperies, and other treatments that are not flat (see page 10).
- The extension to the left (C) and right (D) is the stackback allowance (see below).
- If your treatment will be mounted on traverse rods and open at the center, you'll need to allow for a center overlap as well.
- If your treatment will hang from a mounting board or rod that returns to the wall, you should measure the return and add it to the side extensions (see page 194). The finished length of board-mounted treatments is figured to the top of the board.
- When figuring length for curtains that hang from rings, remember that the top of the curtain will be at the bottom of the rings as they sit on the pole.

allow for the stackback

If your treatment includes panels that will draw open to expose all or most of the glass, the hardware must extend beyond the window at the sides; these extensions, called a stackback allowance, must be ample enough to hold the fabric (see the drawing below). An extension equal to one-third the width of glass you'll expose is usually sufficient; very heavy fabrics may require a larger stackback space. Split the stackback evenly if the curtains open from the middle, place it all on one side if they open from one side.

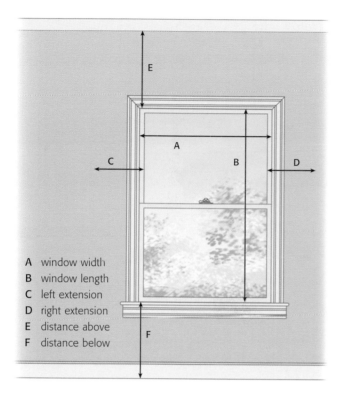

A window width
B window length
C left extension
D right extension
E distance above
F distance below

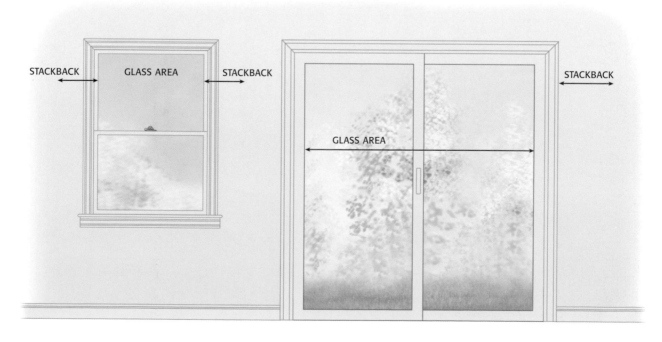

allow for the return to the wall

Finding the size of the return to the wall is straightforward, as shown at right—just measure the depth of the mounting board or the side of a U-shaped rod. Double this measurement and add it to the width across the front of the board or rod (the window width plus side extensions); use the total to calculate the treatment fullness (see page 10).

top treatment proportions

While there are standard guidelines for determining top treatment length, this is frequently a matter of personal preference; the object is to keep it in balance with other elements in the treatment and the overall scale of your décor. Remember that the top of your treatment may be placed above the top of the window. The following rules are classic.

LENGTH FOR TOP TREATMENTS USED ALONE. Top treatments used alone (or over shades, blinds, or similar adjustable window coverings) should have a length equal to one-quarter of the distance from the top of the treatment to the bottom of the windowsill or apron.

LENGTH FOR TOP TREATMENTS USED OVER DRAPERIES OR CURTAINS. Top treatments used over floor-length draperies or curtains should have a length equal to about one-fifth the distance from the top of the treatment to the floor.

For treatments on mounting boards, double the front-to-back measurement and add it to the width of the front. Measure the length from the top of the board.

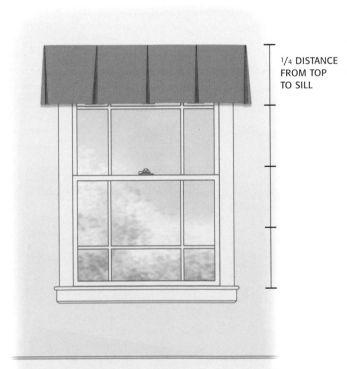

¼ DISTANCE FROM TOP TO SILL

Measure from top to sill and divide by four to find the length of a top treatment used alone.

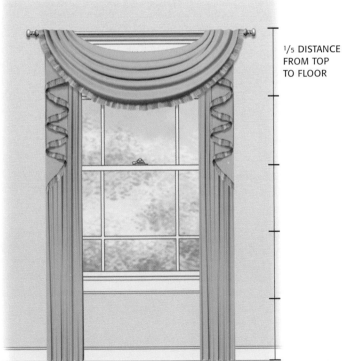

⅕ DISTANCE FROM TOP TO FLOOR

Measure from top to floor and divide by five to find the length of a top treatment used over curtains.

window terms and shapes

Be sure you understand these key words and window shapes—they'll help you make smart decisions when you choose, design, commission, or make a window treatment.

APRON. An applied interior trim piece that runs beneath the window unit, below the sill.

CASEMENT. A window with a frame that hinges on one side, like a door.

CASING. The decorative molding, or trim, around a window.

CLERESTORY. A window high on a wall, often above other windows.

GLAZING. The glass in the window.

GRILLE. A decorative, removable grate that makes a window appear to be made of several small panes of glass.

JAMB. The frame that surrounds and supports the window sash.

LIGHTS. Separately framed panes of glass in a multi-paned window. Energy efficient, double-glazed windows now have simulated multiple panes that are divided by a grille between the glass layers and integral wooden grilles on each outer face of the glass.

MULLION. A vertical trim piece that separates multiple windows.

MUNTIN. A slender strip of wood used to frame the individual panes in a multi-pane window.

SASH. A window frame surrounding glass. Sash may be fixed or operable; a double-hung window has two sashes.

SILL. The interior or exterior shelf below the window sash, at the bottom of the casing.

TRANSOM. A window over a door, or sometimes over another window. May be fixed or operable.

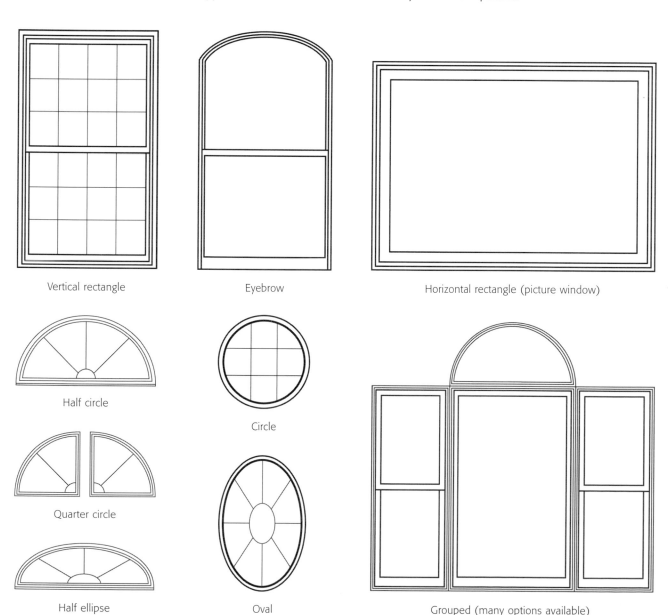

Vertical rectangle

Eyebrow

Horizontal rectangle (picture window)

Half circle

Circle

Quarter circle

Half ellipse

Oval

Grouped (many options available)

fabric facts

It's likely the most striking thing about your window treatments will be the fabric they're made from. Whether you are ordering readymade or custom treatments or sewing your own, an understanding of basic fabric facts will help you select fabric with the desired design effect, durability, and cost. If you plan to make your window fashions, there are books available to walk you through the exact steps of yardage calculation and construction.

fabric has character

There are hundreds of types of fabric that are appropriate for window treatments—gingham, chintz, damask, voile, cheesecloth, brocade, velvet, and denim are just a few. Fabrics for home décor are most often made of cotton, silk, or linen or a blend of these fibers; sheers and lace are usually polyester, nylon, or acetate. There are also innovative modern fabrics made from synthetic fibers and unusual plant fibers such as bamboo. If you are shopping for fabric and aren't sure what type you want, be as descriptive of the desired characteristics as you can when asking your vendor for help—opaque or sheer, patterned or solid, smooth or textured, shiny or matte, crisp or soft, light, medium, or heavyweight. There are many fabric resources on the Internet, and you can learn a lot about the options and naming conventions by exploring them.

Decorator fabrics are created to be efficient to use. They come in generous widths, usually 54 to 60 inches. For the most part, these fabrics are durable, although fragility is inherent in loosely woven fabrics, and almost all fabrics will fade from prolonged exposure to sunlight. Some silk fabrics may deteriorate over time, especially along sharp folds. Decorator fabrics often have finishes that protect them from staining. There are special lining fabrics that provide opacity or warmth; some treatments require a decorative lining as part of their design. Dress-weight and quilting fabrics may be used for window treatments if they have the desired look; they're just not as tough, nor usually as wide, as decorator fabrics.

sample and source

Each type of fabric behaves differently, and it's a good idea to handle a sample and look at it in the room where it will hang before committing to a large purchase. Where you purchase your fabric depends on the source for your window treatment. Readymade treatments are available in limited materials; even so, some vendors offer swatches so you can preview the color and texture. Some decorator fabrics are available only "to the trade," meaning through an interior designer or a fabric retailer who specializes in this kind of yard goods; the latter often has a workroom for producing custom window fashions. Interior designers and most custom workrooms can arrange for you to have swatches or borrow larger samples, often called "memos." Some home centers and furniture vendors offer access to decorator fabrics too, and you can purchase directly from some of the Internet sources. Most chain fabric stores carry select decorator fabrics and, depending on where you live, you may have access to an outlet store.

patterns repeat

Whether printed or woven, all patterned fabrics feature a motif or design that is duplicated consistently over their surface. The interval at which the motif or design is duplicated is called the repeat. Most patterns have a vertical and a horizontal repeat; stripes have one or the other. For most window treatments, the vertical repeat is the only one you need to take into consideration.

When multiple pieces of fabric are sewn together to make a window treatment, or if the treatment features a pair of panels, the bottom of each piece or panel must fall at the same place on the vertical repeat or the overall pattern will be out of alignment. If there is more than one treatment in the room, the pattern repeat should be positioned in the same way on each. It's important to understand the repeat on your fabric because its size affects the amount of fabric required to ensure this alignment.

trims by name

Trims provide a decorative flourish, give a custom look, and accentuate design lines. Many types are available—here's what's meant by their various names.

BRAID. A border of decoratively woven thin cords, usually 1 to 3 inches wide, with two finished edges.

CORD. A rope made of twisted strands of thread or yarn, often used for tiebacks. Lipped cord has a narrow flange that can be inserted into a seam.

FRINGE. A border with strands of yarn or cord on one edge. Types with densely packed, cut threads are called brush fringe. Those with twisted cord are called bullion fringe. Other types include ball fringe (with hanging thread balls) and tassel fringe.

GIMP. A narrow braid, up to about 1/2-inch wide, with looped or scalloped borders.

PIPING. A fabric-covered cord, available in various diameters from 1/4 to 1 inch, with a narrow flange that can be inserted in a seam. Also called welting.

RIBBON. A flat, narrow, woven fabric border, available in numerous widths, colors, patterns, and styles.

TASSEL. A dangling ornament made by binding a cluster of yarn or cord strands at one end. Often, the binding features a covered bead or other dimensional structure. A tassel tieback consists of one or two tassels attached to a cord. A swag tassel is larger and designed to be suspended from a top treatment.

REPEAT SIZE. To find the size of the repeat on your fabric, identify one point in the pattern (such as the tip of a leaf or center of a flower) and mark it with a pin. Then find the next instance of that point and mark it with another pin. The distance between the points is the size of the repeat. If your fabric is patterned with a prominent motif like the flower spray in the drawing below, you (or whoever is making your window treatment) should identify it and decide how to feature it on the window treatment (see "place motifs to advantage," page 200).

Most fabrics are designed with an even repeat, which is a pattern that is centered horizontally and is symmetrical (or nearly so) at the edges, as shown in the drawing at right. When these fabrics are cut into equal lengths across the same point in the vertical repeat and then placed side-by-side, the pattern automatically matches and, once sewn, will continue without interruption.

Some fabrics have a pattern called a drop repeat (shown below right), which repeats diagonally across the width. These patterns are neither centered horizontally nor symmetrical at the fabric edges. When figuring yardage, you must include an extra vertical half-repeat on each length in order to match the pattern at the seams. It's challenging to position a drop repeat so that it frames a window symmetrically.

An even repeat is symmetrical at opposite points on the fabric edges—you can check this by marking a line across the fabric, perpendicular to the edges. The pattern at the ends of the line will mirror or be two halves of a single motif.

The size of the repeat is the interval at which a motif is duplicated (between the pins on this drawing), not the size of the motif itself.

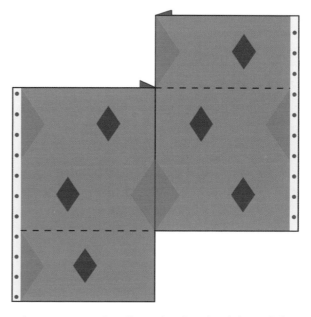

A drop repeat must be offset to be aligned and demands lots of patience.

the math is complex

Calculating yardage requirements for window treatments is complex and, unless you are making your own, you're better off leaving the math to your workroom. If you are making your own, refer to a how-to book that has a yardage worksheet. In either case, you'll be less surprised by the amount required if you understand the principle behind the calculation. In essence, you must add an allowance for a hem at the top and bottom to the visible length of each panel; this total is called the cut length. If the finished panel is to be wider than the width of the fabric, you must allow additional cut lengths as needed to create this width.

If your fabric is patterned, you must also make sure the vertical repeat can be placed consistently on all the panels so that the pattern lines up across all the pieces (plain and lengthwise-striped fabrics don't have a vertical repeat). It's unlikely the repeat will divide evenly into your required cut length; so, in order for each length to begin at the same place in the pattern and thus ensure that the motifs align horizontally, you'll need extra fabric. When this extra is added to the cut length, the total is called the adjusted cut length; to find the total yardage needed, multiply the adjusted cut length by the number of lengths required.

Don't fool yourself into thinking it's not important to align small patterns—misalignments are surprisingly obvious. It doesn't take much extra fabric to align small prints, so don't skimp in this area.

add partial widths at the sides

If whole and partial widths of fabric must be sewn together to create the width needed for your window treatment, the partial width should always be placed at the side of the treatment, where the seam will be less apparent. On wide top treatments such as upholstered cornices, a whole width should usually be centered, with a partial width sewn to each side; the exception to this would be when the top treatment spans several windows and must align with treatments centered in each window below.

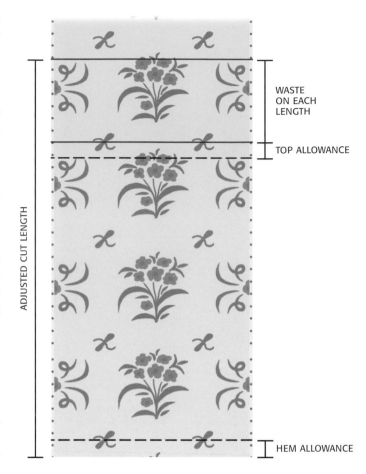

When figuring yardage, include extra "waste" fabric so each panel can begin at the same place in the pattern.

To obtain the needed width for a pair of curtains, piece the panels on opposite edges so that partial widths are at the sides of the window.

color, pattern, and texture

Three important building blocks of window treatment design are color, pattern, and texture. Here are some tips for evaluating and combining these elements to create a pleasing effect that complements your architecture and expresses your taste.

DEVELOP A DESIGN SENSIBILITY. Look through decorating magazines and clip or mark examples of fabrics, window treatments, and rooms that appeal to you. Although they may seem unrelated at first, you'll come to recognize a pattern to your preferences.

KEEP THE WHOLE ROOM IN MIND. It may seem obvious that window fashions should relate to the rest of your décor, and vice versa, but it's easy to lose track of the numerous elements while you focus on the details of just one component.

BEGIN WITH COLORS YOU LIKE. Open your eyes to the natural world and the world of fashion, and note the colors and palettes you find most appealing.

CHOOSE YOUR FOCUS. Window treatments that match the wall color create a background for other items in the room. Treatments that contrast with the wall color capture the eye and take attention away from other elements.

THINK LONG-TERM. Quiet colors may wear better visually than strong ones.

ACKNOWLEDGE THE SUN. Color is affected by the direction of the light. Windows facing south and east let in warm, cheery light. Indirect northern light is softer and cooler. Intense western light is harsher.

CHECK THE LIGHT BY DAY AND NIGHT. Color changes under different light conditions. Tape a sample yard of fabric to the wall and look at it at different times of the day and in lamplight.

EXPECT IMPACT FROM VOLUME. The more there is of a color, the stronger it looks. Bright and offbeat colors may work better as accents than as the principal fabric.

LET COLORS REPEAT. Patterns that share at least one color combine easily, and solid-color fabrics in hues picked up from a pattern enhance visual harmony.

SMALL PATTERNS READ AS TEXTURE. From a distance, you won't discern the detail of a small pattern, you'll just get an overall impression that is livelier than the effect of a solid color.

MEDIUM-SIZE PATTERNS ARE VERSATILE. Their details are easy to see and they don't overwhelm other parts of the décor.

LARGE PATTERNS HAVE POWER AND PITFALLS. They add drama and distinction but may make a small space seem smaller. Plus their details may be lost in the pleats and folds of some treatment styles.

A MIX OF SCALES CREATES INTEREST. Combine small-, medium-, and large-scale patterns in a single treatment or in the overall décor. This is a good strategy whether you're mixing like patterns (three florals) or unlike (two florals and a check).

THREE IS BETTER THAN TWO. A combination of three patterns, or two patterns and a solid, is usually more interesting. If only two patterns are used, choose small and medium, or medium and large; don't combine relative extremes.

DISTRIBUTE PATTERN THROUGHOUT THE SPACE. Placing pattern only at the windows may throw your décor off balance.

CONSIDER THE SURFACE. Whether smooth, coarse, shiny, matte, nubby, velvety, or some combination of these, the surface of a material—whether fabric, wood, vinyl, bamboo, or something else—will reflect or absorb light in different ways. The smoother the surface, the more lustrous the effect.

STRUCTURE CREATES TEXTURE. Blinds and shutters, even when made of smooth materials, have dimensional surfaces. So do open-weave and quilted fabrics. Pleated, gathered, swagged, and layered window treatments add visual texture to the walls—even if the fabric is plain.

TEXTURE ADDS PATTERN. If the weave of a fabric is obvious, it contributes to visual activity in the room. Monochromatic schemes are more interesting if they feature a mix of textures. Texture also enhances schemes that have a mix of solid colors.

TRIMS ARE PART OF THE PICTURE. Braid, fringe, tassels, and other embellishments add color, pattern, and texture to whatever they adorn. Placed thoughtfully, they'll add rhythm to the overall décor and bring specific shapes into focus.

SHEER FABRICS SPREAD COLOR AND TEXTURE. When light filters through sheers, the shadows that are cast add interest to the surroundings. If the sheer fabric has a prominent weave, like lace, or is embroidered, this effect is more pronounced.

HANDLE THE FABRIC. While there are many right fabric choices for every type of window treatment, some kinds of fabric won't be successful for some kinds of treatments. Always handle and manipulate a sample that is large enough for you to determine if the fabric is soft or crisp enough to drape, pleat, gather, or otherwise create the effect you desire. Professionals call this quality the fabric's "hand."

place motifs to advantage

Prominent motifs should be positioned so they are whole at either the top or bottom of the treatment (or in both places if the repeat works out that way). When the fabric is purchased, care should be taken to unroll it, find the point in the pattern chosen for the bottom of the treatment, and measure the hem allowance below it (toward the cut end of the fabric). Once you find this spot, you can measure your yardage from it; as long as the adjusted cut length (see page 198) was figured correctly, there will be enough fabric for the motifs to be placed properly on each length.

there's a convention for every treatment

On curtains and draperies, a whole motif is usually placed just above the bottom edge; this puts any partial motif at the top where it is less noticeable because of the pleats or folds in the fabric. Roller shades usually have a whole motif at the bottom too, where it will be visible unless the shade is raised all the way.

On shades that lift from the bottom, like Roman and cloud styles, a whole motif is usually placed at the top; this puts any partial motif at the bottom where it is concealed in the folds or draped poufs unless the shade is fully lowered.

If a valance is the same fabric as the treatment it tops, the pattern on the fabric is usually positioned to continue vertically without interuption from one layer to the next.

If your fabric has horizontal stripes, be thoughtful about how you position them on your treatment—usually a thicker or darker stripe is placed just above the bottom fold.

For curtains and roller shades, position a complete motif at the bottom; let partial motifs fall at the top.

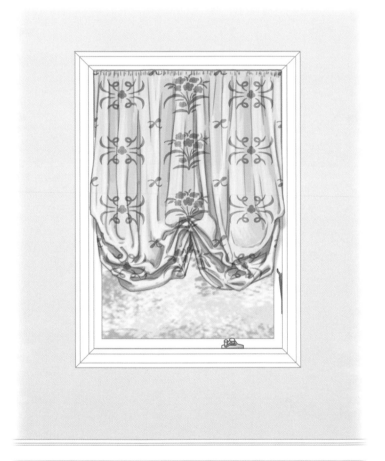

For shades that are raised from the bottom, position a complete motif at the top.

bed furnishings guidelines

The steps to planning bed furnishings really depend on the design of the bed, but most bed coverings and many hangings are quite straightforward to visualize and plan. When working out hangings, make sure the design is structured correctly for attachment to the specific frame. For coverings, be sure to plan how the fabric will fit around posts or inside a footboard; the corners of bed skirts and spreads may need to split to fit around these.

plan hangings like curtains

Most bed hangings can be planned the same way you plan curtains and valances—just measure the length from the top of the frame and the width between the posts. Canopies, especially for four-poster beds, can be very complicated and most should be left to a professional. Hangings that attach to crowns are just curtains; the fact that the frame is round doesn't affect the panels as long as the frame is parallel to the floor.

Some bed frames come apart easily, making it possible to slide rod pocket, tab, or eyelet curtains onto the rails. But others don't; for these, you'll want to use curtains that attach with ties. And some frames are meant to have the top treatment or the panels tacked right to the wood—sometimes under a decorative molding.

measure twice for bed coverings

Once in each direction, that is—from the head to the foot and from side to side—measuring from hemline to hemline in each case.

Bedspreads extend to the floor; coverlets extend at least an inch or two below the bottom of the mattress, to cover the top of the bed skirt, and may be somewhat longer if you wish. (The portion of the cover that hangs over the sides is called the drop.) For a pillow tuck, add 12 to 18 inches to the length.

For a bed skirt (also called a dust ruffle), measure the length and width of the box spring. These are the dimensions of the cover to which the skirt will be sewn. Measure the length from the top of the box spring to the floor. Plan the skirt like a valance or curtain, making the total width after pleating or gathering sufficient to wrap around the bed from head to head across the foot (twice the length plus the width of the box spring). If the bed frame has legs that are both sturdy and attractive, you can alternatively place tension rods between them and put an individual skirt on each rod—but be sure to make the coverlet long enough to cover the rod.

remember the accessories

Duvets and pillows come in standard sizes (with many options for throw pillows); generally their covers should have the same dimensions. You may think you can create throw pillow covers from scraps of a companion curtain or coverlet, but they take more fabric than you'd expect, so it's a good idea to allot specific yardage for them when you are planning. This is doubly true if you want to center a fabric motif on the pillow face or use a stripe for a ruffle. Don't forget to plan closures and trimmings for these accessories.

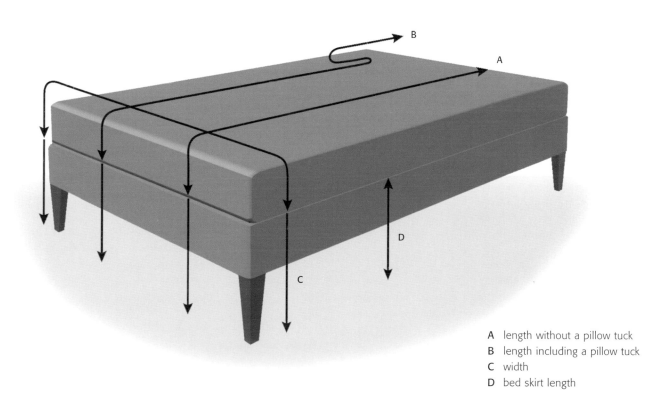

A length without a pillow tuck
B length including a pillow tuck
C width
D bed skirt length

treatments for challenging windows

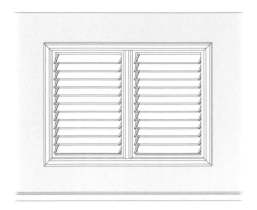

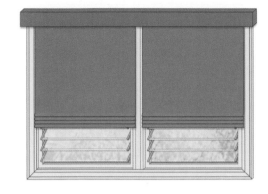

JALOUSIE WINDOWS have glass louvers that tilt into the room when open, making it difficult to hang a treatment flush against them. To work around this, hang curtains or a cloud shade on a rod that returns to the wall at the sides, or hang a flat treatment from the front of a cornice.

A cornice with a Roman shade that clears the open louvers

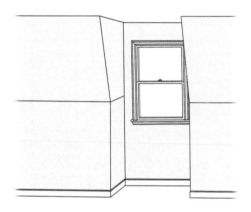

DORMER WINDOWS are usually tucked tightly between perpendicular walls, sometimes under a slanted ceiling. You can use a modestly proportioned version of most window treatments in a dormer; just remember you won't be able to pull curtains off to the sides.

Curtains fixed over the window and tied open at the sides

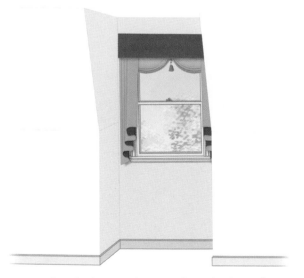

A roll-up shade hung above a bookcase under the window

A swag-skirted valance set between the projecting walls

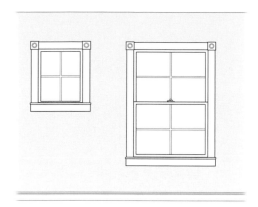

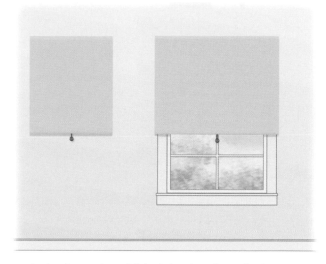

MISMATCHED WINDOWS have a tendency to call attention to themselves. To minimize this, hang matching floor-length treatments on both or choose a simple covering that matches or gently blends with the wall color; consider fabric that matches the wallpaper.

Shades that are just slightly darker than the wall color

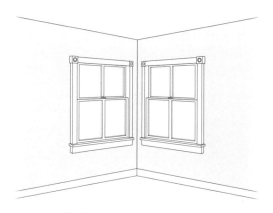

CORNER WINDOWS may be dressed with a single outside mounted treatment or with a pair of inside or outside mounted coverings. Which you choose may depend on how close the windows are to one another. Use an angled rod if the windows are close to the corner.

Adjacent sheer curtains flanked by opaque curtains

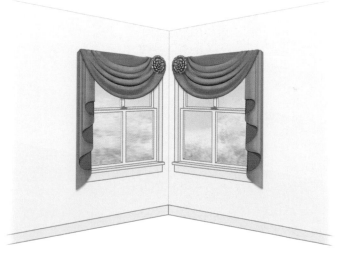

A pair of outside mounted cloud shades

A pair of swags, each with a single cascade on the outer side

treatments for challenging windows

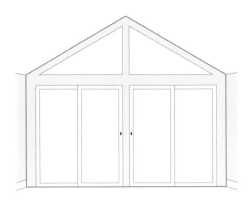

CATHEDRAL WINDOWS are usually part of a window wall or placed above glass doors and, if a covering is desired, should be dressed as part of an ensemble with their neighbors. Electrical controls are available to operate shades and blinds that are out of reach; for shutters you'll need a pole.

Top-down horizontal blinds above sliding doors with individual blinds under a single valance

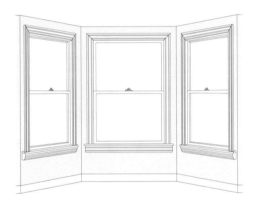

BAY WINDOWS dressed individually look taller than those flanked with panels at the ends only. But the view is more expansive when there are no curtains between the windows—the same is true for bow windows, which have abutting windows. Contoured rods are available for use in a bow or a bay with closely spaced windows.

Pairs of floor-length rod pocket curtains, each separated by a rod sleeve, over roller shades

A pair of curtains with tiebacks on a pole across the bay window alcove, with sash curtains on each window

London shades, outside mounted on each window; inside mounts are another option

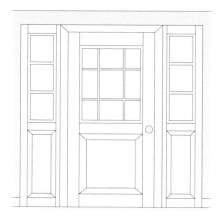

ENTRY DOORS WITH SIDE LIGHTS present conflicting needs for privacy and daylight. Sheer treatments offer modest amounts of both. Opaque fabrics provide more privacy and a little light may filter in around their edges. Adjustable shutters and blinds offer total privacy but may be out of keeping with some decorating styles.

Matching sheer sash curtains over a glass insert on an entry door and side lights

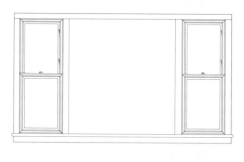

PICTURE WINDOWS containing one large window flanked by two small ones work well with three matching treatments that move individually under a single top treatment. Or minimize the uneven proportions with a valance and draperies opened to expose only part of each side window.

Mini-blinds, which virtually disappear when fully raised, under a graceful, wrapped swag

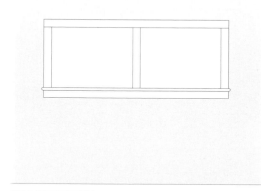

WIDE, SHORT WINDOWS placed high on the wall often look out of balance, an effect that is worsened when they're flanked by floor-length curtains. Inside mounted shades or blinds break up the expanse; a wide piece of furniture below the window will make the overall effect less awkward.

Horizontal blinds in each window, balanced by a daybed against the wall

index